After reading mechanical sciences at Cambridge, A. H. A. H
gained practical research and experience in civil engineering, and
became a Lecturer in that subject at Newcastle and, later, Cambridge University. While at Newcastle he also qualified as a Town
Planner. In 1949 he was appointed Secretary to the Royal Commission on Wales and Monmouthshire, remaining in that post until
his retirement in 1973.

He has travelled mainly in France, but has also visited Spain,
Czechoslovakia and Yugoslavia, studying hill-forts in all those
countries; and publishing descriptions of forts in France and Spain.
His own excavations, mostly in Wales, have been on a small scale,
to investigate particular problems; but he has assisted on several
major excavations both in Britain and France.

He was awarded the CBE in 1973 and in 1974 was awarded a
D.Litt.(hon. causa) by the University of Wales. A Fellow of the
Society of Antiquaries of London, and also that of Scotland, he was
President of the Cambrian Archaeological Association for 1972.

A. H. A. HOGG

A Guide to the Hill-Forts of Britain

Granada Publishing

Paladin Books
Granada Publishing Ltd
8 Grafton Street, London W1X 3LA

Published by Paladin Books 1984

First published in Great Britain by
Hart-Davis, MacGibbon Ltd 1975

ISBN 0-586-08460-6

Reproduced, printed and bound in Great Britain by
Hazell Watson & Viney Limited,
Aylesbury, Bucks

Set in Photon Times

To my wife

Contents

Acknowledgements

I am greatly indebted to the following individuals, both for permission to utilize their original plans (the numbers of the relevant figures are given in parentheses), and for suggestions and unpublished information: Mr J. Collis (54); Mr D. Coombs (85); Mr R. W. Feachem (12, 20, 22, 44, 102); Mr J. Forde-Johnston (71); Lady Fox (51, 86); Mr P. S. Gelling; Mrs C. M. Guido (28, 79); Professor C. F. C. Hawkes (31); Mrs T. C. Hencken (29); Mr R. F. Jessup (25); Mr G. Jobey (107); Dr K. M. Kenyon (98, 105); Mr A. King; Professor S. Piggott (81, 106); Miss K. M. Richardson (26); Dr H. N. Savory (57); Mr A. Sorrell; Dr S. C. Stanford (13, 55); Dr K. Steer (80); Professor W. J. Varley (18, 89); Dr J. B. Ward-Perkins (88); Sir Mortimer Wheeler (11, 84, 97); Miss M. Whitley (48); and Dr A. E. Wilson. I am also grateful to the following institutions: the Ordnance Survey (1–3, 14–16); the Royal Commissions on Ancient and Historical Monuments: for England (55, 74, 77, 93); for Scotland (59, 67, 80, 95, 103); and for Wales and Monmouthshire (37, 4, 52, 56, 72, 75, 91, 92); and to the Victoria County History of England (35, 36, 38, 65); and also to the secretaries and editors of the following societies: the Society of Antiquaries of London (49, 50); the Society of Antiquaries of Scotland (47, 70); the Royal Archaeological Institute; the Cambrian Archaeological Association (68, 71, 82); the Devon Archaeological Society (76); the Wiltshire Archaeological and Natural History Society (69); also all those mentioned individually in the gazetteer.

The aerial photographs have been supplied by the Committee for Aerial Photography, of the University of Cambridge, by courtesy of Professor J. K. St Joseph, director. Copyright is reserved.

The finished plans are by Mr C. Baker and the reconstructions by Mr Dylan Roberts, from pencil drafts by the author.

List of Figures

List of Plates

Preface and Definitions

No archaeologist is satisfied with the term 'hill-fort', but all the alternatives which have been suggested are open to even more objections, so it will be used without further apology, sometimes even shortened to 'fort'. As will be seen later, if 'fort' is understood in the modern sense this is misleading: the enclosures may have corresponded to anything from a cattle kraal to a small town, but were seldom exclusively military. If a formal definition is demanded, a hill-fort may be described as an enclosure, apparently fortified, and so placed as to gain some defensive advantage from its position; as being of a type generally built during the native Iron Age; and as normally not less than 0·2 hectare in enclosed area. The restriction on date is to exclude structures such as neolithic causewayed camps or medieval earthwork castles, and that on area to separate out the recognizably different fortifications known as 'brochs' and 'duns' in Scotland. Brochs and duns are in fact contemporary with hill-forts but are on average very much smaller; they are arbitrarily excluded as a matter of convenience, to limit the field covered.

Hill-forts, then, are enclosures with ramparts built (mostly) by prehistoric man to protect his settlements or stock. These ramparts are now reduced to grassy banks or heaps of rubble, but are still conspicuous features of the countryside in many parts of Britain. Every year, new discoveries throw light on the nature of these 'hill-forts' and on the way of life of their builders, so that any attempt at a detailed definitive study of them falls out of date faster than it can be written. Nevertheless the great mass of information which has been collected does permit a fairly clear general idea of what these places were like in their prime, and when and why they were built.

This book is not a text book, and makes no attempt to summarize all work that has been done on British hill-forts; still less does it cover the Iron Age as a whole. So, although it is hoped that the collection of material may be of use to specialists, it is primarily intended for those who find that their enjoyment of the countryside is enhanced by reconstructing the past in imagination. Even companions who do not share this interest will usually find the view from a hill-fort rewarding. No footnotes are given, but for the sake of those who wish to pursue the subject the chief sources are listed in a biblio-graphy.

The main body of the book falls into two parts. The first deals with the various elements of hill-fort structure, with sufficient background to enable the reader to place them in their historical and social context, while the second, the gazetteer, describes a representative selection of hill-forts distributed throughout the country. All sites, British or foreign, which are mentioned in the first section are included, so the second section provides the necessary references and other details, and forms an index.

Some readers may regret, or even resent, the use of metric measure-ments, but it would have been pedantic to cling to feet and inches after they have ceased to be the official system. Since the use of dimensions in a general work of this kind is merely to give a rough mental impression of size, it is sufficient to visualize a metre as a 'long yard', a hectare as $2\frac{1}{2}$ acres and a square kilometre as two-fifths of a square mile; more exact factors are 3·281 feet, 2·47 acres and 0·386 square mile. For smaller dimensions, 30 centimetres corre-sponds closely to 1 foot; and, for the benefit of cricketers, 20 metres is the length of a pitch, within 5 inches.

One further explanation is needed. At several hill-forts excavations are either in progress or have only just been completed. I have tried to avoid reference to these, even though the work is naturally of great importance; for not only does it seem undesirable to forestall the excavator with an ill-digested summary of his results, but their full significance cannot really be understood until they have received definitive publication.

Author's Preface to the Paladin Edition

Much important work has been published relating to hill-forts since 1975, but cannot be incorporated in the text of this edition, which is necessarily a straightforward reprint, apart from a few verbal corrections; the scales given in Fig. 17 are now slightly incorrect, owing to the change in page size. Even where further work has been done on individual sites, the descriptions and references have had to be left unaltered.

Most of the text remains valid, but some recent publications are noted below, especially those which substantially alter views expressed in 1975. The selection is very restricted, and much work of fully equal importance has been excluded owing to lack of space for discussion. Bibliographical abbreviations used are given on pages 103–4.

First in importance, for anyone seriously interested in the subject, is the second (1978) edition of Cunliffe's *Iron Age Communities in Britain* (Archaeology in Britain series, Routledge). The work is a general study of the period, but includes descriptions and illustrations of many hill-forts. In addition, a list of relevant radiocarbon dates is given. These, in conjunction with an extended study of pottery and other objects, are beginning to provide a reasonably sound chronology; but the rough approximations used here (see especially pp. 28–9) remain adequate for the general reader. Here also attention may be drawn once again to D. W. Harding (Editor), *Hill-forts* . . . (see p. 111), which owing to the date of its publication did not receive in 1975 the emphasis which its importance merits; M. Avery's opening chapter, 'A Student's Introduction,' is particularly valuable.

General Topographical Information (p. 106) is now supplemented by A. H. A. Hogg, *British Hill-forts; an Index.* (BAR British Series 62, 1979) which lists all hill-forts on the mainland known to the compiler at that date, with indexes, grid coordinates and selective bibliographical references, but no plans or descriptions. The three Ancient Monuments Commissions have continued their work: England; Gloucestershire and the Cotswolds (1976), and Northamptonshire, with few hill-forts (4 vols. 1975–82). Scotland; Argyll (Kintyre, 1, 1971, and Lorn, 2, 1975). Wales; Glamorgan (vol. 1, pt. 2, 1976) and Brecknockshire complete as to fieldwork.

The remaining changes in viewpoint arise from work on individual sites. In 1975, the term hill-fort was defined to exclude structures of Neolithic date; but at that time R. J. Mercer had not completed his work on Carn Brea (pp. 161–4). His report (*Cornish Archaeology* No. 20 (1981) 1–204) shows that although there was some Iron Age occupation on the site, at least the inner ramparts enclosing the knolls carrying the Monument and the Castle, some 4 hectares, are almost certainly Neolithic; and he draws attention to other known or probable fortified sites of that period. Some hill-forts, therefore, are of Neolithic origin, though without excavation they cannot be distinguished with certainty from Iron Age examples.

The other major change in outlook concerns the interiors of hill-forts. Graeme Guilbert ('Planned Hillfort Interiors', *Proc. Prehistoric Soc.* (41 (1975) 203–221) has demonstrated that in some cases distinct zones are allocated to different types of buildings. Moel y Gaer, Rhosesmor, Flintshire (SJ 211 690) is the best-studied example. This is a roughly circular enclosure of 2·7 hectares, generally bivallate. About a sixth of the area has been excavated, and *if this is representative* it suggests that an annular space about 25 metres wide within the rampart was restricted to four-post buildings, while in the central area bands, apparently radial, were alternately devoted to round buildings and to more 'four-posters'. This was in the second phase of occupation, probably in the 6th century B.C. Whether the extrapolation from the excavated area is legitimate or not, there is clear evidence for deliberate planning. Similarly at Danebury (p. 185; 2nd and 3rd interim reports, *Ant. J.* LVI (1976) 198–216; LXI (1981) 238–254), to quote from p. 250 of the third report: "in a period of major reorganisation, probably towards the end of the fourth century, the southern part of the fort . . . was replanned with rows of storage structures served by metalled roads . . ." It seems now to be the general consensus of opinion, that with rare exceptions these rectangular four- and six-post settings correspond to buildings for storage, probably of grain. Comments on these buildings, especially as regards the interior of Croft Ambrey (pp. 100–1), need reconsideration, and the reconstruction drawing of that fort (pl. 7) is probably misleading. The rows of small square buildings shown were probably interspersed with large areas where buildings were exclusively round; these were not found owing to the accident of partial excavation.

One misunderstanding displayed by some reviewers of the 1975 edition ought perhaps to be eliminated. The Gazetteer is essentially subsidiary to the first part of the book. Its primary function is to avoid the need to interrupt the general account by inserting references or descriptions which are not immediately relevant at that point; it is for that reason that the four foreign hill-forts are included. The secondary objective is, so far as possible, to provide any reader, wherever resident, with a sample of representative and accessible hill-forts.

Any such selection will inevitably be liable to regretful second thoughts, so the opportunity will be taken to mention two exceptionally noteworthy forts in Aberdeenshire: Mither Tap of Bennachie (NJ 683 224; described in Feachem, *Preh. Scot.*, P. 104), and Tap o' Noth (NJ 485 293; *Preh. Scot.*, p.106). Both are more than a mile from, and 1000 ft above, the nearest road (a factor which contributed to their omission in 1975), but the ascents are not at all difficult and are well repaid.

1
Names

Of the two thousand or more hill-forts in Britain, only one or two retain their original names in recognizable form; neither can now be interpreted. One is The Wrekin, anciently Uriconion; in Roman times the name was transferred to the new city, now Wroxeter, but has since returned to its original site. Old Sarum, too, has not departed far from its original Sorviodunon. A few others can be inferred with reasonable certainty. Almondbury, Yorkshire, was Camulodunon, the stronghold of Camulos the god of war, who also gave his name to Colchester. Less certainly, Ingleborough may have been Rigodunon, 'the royal stronghold'. At others, the ancient name may survive in a more or less corrupt form. It is an attractive suggestion, for example, that both Breedon-on-the-Hill and Bredon are derived from Brigodunon, which translates almost literally into 'hill-fort'; but there are not enough early forms of the names for proof.

Most names were either forgotten or irretrievably altered during the period of the Roman occupation and the subsequent breakdown of social order, which seems to have extended over the whole country. When the places are mentioned again it is usually as land— marks, not as inhabited sites. The people who renamed them felt no doubt as to their original use. The enclosure was a 'burgh', a 'dun', a 'caer', 'urbs antiqua', 'veterum castrum', almost always implying a fortified permanent settlement. These identifications, by people whose way of life was not very unlike that of the builders, weigh heavily against the doubts which some modern archaeologists have expressed as to the function of the forts. Most of the names given, however, are either merely descriptive or indicative of ownership. They are of the same type in all parts of the country.

The earliest references occur in boundary surveys appended to pre-Norman charters. Bredon Hill, for example, is first mentioned as a 'city with the ancient name of Baenintesbury', meaning 'Baening's fort', a name preserved in that of the Banbury Stone which stands on the hill. Chastleton Barrow, is 'the hill of Susibre, an ancient city'. The name is Celtic; the last element 'bre' means 'hill', but the meaning of the first is uncertain. Salmonsbury is 'a city called Sulemonnes-bury', which has nothing to do with Solomon or fish, but means the 'ploughman's fort'. Examples can be multiplied almost indefinitely. To cite a few of them: Almondsbury, Gloucestershire, is 'Aethelmund's fort', but Almondbury, Yorkshire is 'All-man's-bury', a fort publicly owned; Hembury, is Hean-burh, the 'high fort'; Membury is Maen-burh, the 'stone fort'. Comparable names are found in Scotland. Dunmore, the 'big fort', is common; Dunsapie, near Arthur's Seat, means the fort covered with tufts of grass; Dundurn does in fact resemble a fist from some aspects.

Names which could have been given when the place was in use are uncommon, but do occur. Winklebury was Winterburge, a 'strong-hold used in winter'. Traprain Law was formerly Dunpelder, the 'fort of the palisades' − though excavation suggests that all the defences were of stone. Nevertheless, since this translation is explicable as a simple description it is to be preferred to the alternative 'fort of the spear shafts', which would fall into the same class as some which hint tantalizingly at forgotten folk tales, like Castell Nadolig ('Christmas Castle'); Old Winchester Hill, which stands 20 kilometres from Winchester; or Dun na Ban-Oige, the 'fort of the rich woman' − or perhaps 'of the young wife'. Maiden Castle in archaeological contexts almost always refers to the Dorset hill-fort, but the name is quite common and widespread. Derivation from 'Celtic' *Mai-dun* has been proposed, but this is fanciful. Another suggestion is that the fortresses so named were impregnable; but by the far most probable explanation is that these sites were known locally as places where one might hope to meet young women who were not.

More interesting names are those which even in their earliest forms contain some reference to a known mythical or historical character. There is a strong temptation, to which many archaeologists have succumbed at some time, to accept an apparent tradition of this kind at its face value. Some, indeed, may be genuine; but there are enough examples where even early identifications are demonstrably false to cast doubt on all the others.

The proliferation of 'Caesar's Camps' seems to have begun in the seventeenth century, but as early as 1279 the rampart on Bindon Hill was identified as Julius Caesar's dyke. Caer Helen, the older name of

Pen-y-Gaer above Llanbedr-y-Cennin, implies that the fort belonged to the wife of Magnus Maximus. These were reasonable attempts to link history with visible monuments. Similarly, storytellers have given verisimilitude to their tales by linking them to real places. The composer of the Mabinogion tale of Math and Mathonwy has associated Dinlle, 'Lleu's stronghold', with a mythical or imaginary character Lleu Llaw Gyffes, 'Lleu of the deft hand'. The whole of this story is woven round local place-names and topographical features; for example, it gives an account of the theft of pigs which is clearly based on a run of 'moch' (pig) place-names, and it explains a naturally-holed stone, which still exists, as having been pierced by Lleu's spear. So it seems likely that Lleu Llaw Gyffes is essentially an invention of the story-teller, whereas the Lleu after whom the fort was named may have been just as real as the Aethelmund who owned Almondsbury.

Examples of this kind cast doubt on the validity of apparently traditional identifications, and indeed it seems safer to reject them all, except as indicating interesting possibilities. The sort of evidence which would be needed to carry reasonable conviction is discussed below, when considering Dinas Emrys and South Cadbury.

As would be expected, names which hint at the survival of genuine folk memories occur almost exclusively in 'Celtic' areas. In Wales we have Dinorwig, of the Ordovices, and Dinllaen, of the Leinstermen; in Scotland Dunearn, Dumbarton, Dumyat and Dunkeld incorporate some recollection of Irishmen, Britons, Maeatae and Caledonians — the last two are tribes recorded by Roman historians as having fought against Severus. Even if these are genuine traditional names and not the result of early attempts at historical identification, the question remains as to whether they imply particularly important places within the territory of the people named, or whether they correspond to strongholds established outside their own regions. Further, in attempting to assess the possible age of such names, it is relevant that in all records *known* to originate earlier than about the fourth century AD the *dunon* element occurs *after* the descriptive term.

Associations with historical or semi-historical characters are at least equally open to suspicion. Dunsinane does in fact contain the foundations of an early medieval castle which could have belonged to Macbeth, though the surrounding earthworks are far older. At Old Oswestry none of the pottery is now regarded as post-Roman, so there is nothing except the name Caer Ogyrfan to imply occupation by King Arthur's father-in-law King Gogyrfan, if indeed he ever existed outside the minds of story tellers; but Dinas Emrys was not only fortified at about the time of Ambrosius Aurelianus, it also enclosed a curious pool and associated structures which agree remarkably well with the legend attached to the site (see pp. 186, 188).

Except perhaps at Dunsinane, these traditional associations will not really stand up to critical study. We do not know if any forts near Old Oswestry would display post-Roman occupation, and even the detailed agreement of the curious legend attached to Dinas Emrys with the results of excavation could be explained by assuming that the story was made up to account for features visible there.

Another Arthurian association, recorded in the first half of the sixteenth century, makes Barry Hill at Alyth in Perthshire the place of imprisonment of Guinevere after Arthur's death. No one in modern times has taken this very seriously, but a rather later 'tradition' has led to excavations of archaeological importance. It provides a good example of the difficulty of evaluating such evidence.

Leland, at the end of the sixteenth century, records as a local belief that South Cadbury Castle was the site of Camelot, where King Arthur held his court; and twentieth-century excavations, carried out with great care and skill, have shown that the hill-fort was indeed a place of major importance at the right date. At first sight, the agreement of tradition and reality seems all that could be hoped for, establishing the location of Camelot beyond doubt.

Some highly respected archaeologists have accepted the identification, and all must feel grateful that King Arthur's posthumous patronage assisted such a valuable piece of research. Nevertheless, as the excavator has pointed out, the name Camelot is the invention of a French romancer working seven centuries after Arthur's time; and its attribution to South Cadbury, whether by Leland or by his informants, seems to rest on no stronger foundation than the presence nearby of two villages called Queen Camel and West Camel. That South Cadbury was refortified, to become an important centre at about the time when Arthur is likely to have lived, is no longer open to question; but there is no proof that he ruled in this region. Neither is it certain, as yet, that the refortification of South Cadbury is exceptional. Excavations in adjacent hill-forts are for the most part lacking, so the regional background is obscure.

Other characters, with a clearer historical background than

Arthur, have been allotted hill-forts by local enthusiasts. Julius Caesar is the most versatile claimant, starting as already noted with Bindon Down in the thirteenth century – a reasonable identification given the state of knowledge at the time. Later he collected six prehistoric forts, ranging from Farnham to Rotherham, as well as two Norman earth and timber castles, one above Folkestone, the other at Wollaston; and in the seventeenth century, Cissbury was known locally as Caesar's Hill. Two other Romans have been commemorated in this way, but only with one hill-fort apiece. Vespasian's Camp still appears on the map, būt that of Chlorus has reverted to its older name of Figsbury.

Now that the nature of the Roman camp is better known, these identifications can be dismissed at once, but 'Caer Caradoc' offers a more difficult problem. According to Tacitus, Caratacus did occupy what was apparently some sort of hill-fort before his last battle against the Romans, and one might expect its remains to be identifiable. Three earthworks now carry the appropriate name, near Clun, Church Stretton and Llanfihangl-Glyn-Myfry; the first identification was made by William Camden in his *Britannia* (London, 1586). These three hill-forts have one feature in common: they cannot possibly be the place in question, for according to Tacitus the Britons were numerous enough to cause anxiety to two Roman legions, and were accompanied by their families. It is known that two legions, fighting men only, encamped with military precision and economy of space, required 25 hectares, so the real Caer Caradoc must be at least as large; the biggest of the three pretenders only encloses a tenth of that area.

2
Modern Research

The body of archaeological knowledge is built up of items of varying reliability which have been collected more or less at random over a considerable period. Even where an investigation has formed part of a planned programme, this has almost always depended on the initiative of a single individual, and circumstances have seldom allowed it even to approach completion. There are compensating advantages, for archaeology in Britain has escaped the imposition of a rigid hierarchical structure, and no 'authority', however well established, is quite secure against critical appraisal of his work; but few if any branches of the subject have developed in a simple rational way.

None the less, in describing the development of modern research, it is convenient to formulate a logical approach as an ideal against which actual progress can be described. Such a theoretical programme would fall naturally into the following phases:

(a) All known structures regarded as hill-forts would be identified, and their generalized distribution plotted.
(bi) Broad regional varieties would be separated out on the evidence of major obvious characteristics such as size, spacing or number of ramparts and (bii) more complete descriptive surveys, with plans, of groups of forts would be provided.
(c) Accurate detailed surveys would be prepared, and hence the structural development worked out so far as this can be known from surface evidence. The most important objective at this stage would be to identify recognizable types.
(d) Selected typical sites would then be examined by excavation, one or two of each being treated on a large scale, a selection of the remainder being tested to see whether their apparent similarities were genuine.
(e) Finally, the apparently exceptional structures would be in-

vestigated, to discover how they fitted into the general background.

No subject has ever followed such an ideally logical path of development, and the study of hill-forts could not have done so, for interpretation of surface evidence often depends on knowledge of the results of excavation elsewhere. It must be emphasized that the use of this theoretical programme as a basis is imposing an appearance of orderly progress which is illusory.

Thanks to the founders of the Ordnance Survey, in particular General Roy, the theoretical stage (a) is in fact complete, or very nearly so. Until recently, the 6 inch to the mile OS maps represented, as accurately as the scale allowed, all known earthworks. Owing to government-enforced economies, all features on recent editions of these maps and on their 1/10000 successors have been coarsened and generalized, so that even such clearly defined details as the outlines of buildings are no longer faithfully portrayed, and earthworks have suffered with the rest, but the 1/2500 maps still provide accurate basic plans. They are available for much of Britain (though expensive) and the older editions of both these and the '6-inch' are available in libraries.

Detailed local research in the field and aerial photography continue to add occasional hill-forts to those recorded on the maps, but it is unlikely that as many as 10 per cent of the total remain unknown. British archaeologists are thus in the uniquely fortunate position of having available reasonably accurate plans of some 90 per cent or more of all the hill-forts which ever existed in this country, together with large-scale maps permitting a study of their topographical background. The potential riches of this immense mine of information have scarcely been touched, but the Ordnance Survey have placed archaeologists still further in their debt by publication of their Map of Southern Britain in the Iron Age. This, with much other information, shows the distribution of all known hill-forts, partly classified by size and partly by whether their ramparts are single or multiple. The size classes are: less than 1·2 hectares, 1·2–6 hectares, and larger. A similar map is in preparation for northern Britain.

S. C. Stanford, in his discussion of Croft Ambrey (q.v.), has utilized the data on the Iron Age map to distinguish several separate regions, but systematic numerical study of distributions, leading to stage (bi), has scarcely begun. Fairly detailed descriptive regional studies (bii), on the other hand, have been characteristic of British archaeology from an early stage.

One of the best, R. Colt Hoare's *Ancient Wiltshire*, even preceded the publication of the OS maps, and still provides the only collection of hill-fort plans for that county. A later individual pioneer was D. Christison, who almost single-handed covered the greater part of Scotland at the end of the last century. The first organized attempt to cover one country systematically, however, had to await the initiation, soon after 1900, of the Victoria County History (VCH) for England. With few exceptions, the volumes of this splendid work include descriptions of the earthworks in every English county, accompanied by plans to uniform rational scales, mostly 1/5000. The plans are generally based, with little revision, on the Ordnance Survey, and the descriptions do not aim at any analysis of the sequence of development; but as most of the work was done during the first decade of this century, or soon after, it would be unreasonable to expect more.

In 1908 the survey of antiquities of all kinds was given official support by the formation of the three Royal Commissions on Ancient and Historical Monuments. They are concerned to record all types of 'monument', and their work is necessarily slow, since their aim is to be definitive and the number of places which have to be inspected is very large. For a single Welsh county, a recent Inventory contained eighteen hundred entries, but its preparation necessitated the investigation of nearly seven thousand possibly ancient structures.

So far as hill-forts are concerned, the earlier Inventories were generally illustrated by plans based on the 1/2500 maps fairly extensively improved by fieldwork and redrawn – often with an elaborately ornate background which must have involved more labour than the plan itself. Recently, the plans are almost always the result of an original *ad hoc* survey.

A really careful and accurate survey (stage (c) above) can be almost as informative as an excavation – which, indeed, it should always precede – and the detailed study necessary to its preparation will often suggest interpretations which would otherwise have been overlooked. Some of the particular triumphs of surface survey have involved the recognition of unfinished hill-forts. Ladle Hill is the classic example.

This seems to be an appropriate point to comment on one very regrettable modern development. As noted above, the VCH plans were reproduced, almost without exception, to a rational scale such as 1/5000 or 1/2500. Of late this excellent practice has been increasingly abandoned, not through any fault of the surveyors but because some editors and printers have the impertinence deliberately to disregard the author's instructions, thinking some other ratio to page size will look prettier. This viciously innumerate arrogance is often more harmful than would be the deliberate insertion of grammatical errors; for the direct comparison of plans *to a consistent set of scales* can be more instructive than many pages of print.

One must be thankful that excavation (stage (d)) has not in fact had to wait its logical turn; it would have been unbearably tantalizing to have no clue as to what lies beneath the turf. Unrecorded digging for treasure or for lesser 'finds' to add to collections goes back a long way, and even research excavation has its beginnings in the nineteenth century, though its practitioners were rare. Young's work at Burghead may be mentioned.

Many essentials of modern techniques were developed just before 1900, by General Pitt-Rivers. His own generation, and the next, remained uninfluenced, but in the 1920s a number of young men rediscovered or re-invented a scientific approach. The basic principles were to plan the excavations to answer specific questions, and to record with meticulous accuracy the positions of all relics and the fullest possible details of stratification. The structural development of the defences could thus be worked out, in relation to the potentially datable objects found; and an approximately dated sequence could be established for types of pottery and other artifacts.

This approach did not necessarily involve large-scale excavation. To select one example: E. C. Curwen organized a series of investigations in the hill-forts of the Sussex Downs which in a decade produced a reliable framework for the history of the whole region during the Iron Age. The initiative of the Hampshire Field Club in organizing a series of excavations under the direction of C. F. C. Hawkes extended this knowledge over much of the southern chalklands. Even earlier first-rate work was being carried out in Wales by Willoughby Gardner, though his most important piece of research, at Dinorben, had to wait until the sixties for definitive publication.

Small-scale excavations, though, have the weakness that they provide relatively little comparative material and are not very informative as to the social and economic background. To remedy this, and to set knowledge of the southern British Iron Age on a sound basis, something more ambitious was needed. In the mid-1930s Dr (now Sir) Mortimer Wheeler, then director of the Institute of Archaeology, worked out a carefully integrated campaign.

The central feature of this was the large-scale excavation of Maiden Castle near Dorchester, the most impressive hill-fort in southern Britain. This was to be supplemented by a survey of the forts of the whole of northern France, with fairly extensive excavation of selected sites, and excavation of other south British forts near Maiden Castle.

To be effective, this sort of planned campaign, and large-scale excavation of the type undertaken at Maiden Castle, calls for the rare association of exceptional ability in organization and leadership with personal skill in the techniques of excavation and interpretation. Dr Wheeler combined all these requirements with a flair for the best type of publicity, which did much to raise archaeology in public esteem.

Only a small part of the fruits of this brilliantly planned and executed campaign could be harvested, though, for the events of 1939 intervened. On the last day scheduled for the excavations at Duclair by the Seine, a portable radio on the site gave the news of the German invasion of Poland. The Maiden Castle report, published in 1941, was, to quote Sir Mortimer's preface, 'the salvage of the report that should have been'; and although the finds had been recorded with meticulous care, when the opportunity for research returned they had been irretrievably shuffled by the disturbances of wartime. Even so, all subsequent investigation of the Iron Age in southern Britain, and of the nature and function of the hill-forts there, depends heavily on this programme of research.

As yet no other wide-ranging campaign comparable to this has been brought to completion, but there have been several postwar excavations at least equal in scale and quality to that at Maiden Castle. There have also been advances in details of technique, such as the abolition of balks in area excavation, and the use of much broader rampart sections. On some sites which have never been disturbed the meticulous plotting of literally every pebble exposed has revealed information which would have been overlooked by methods used only ten years ago; while on others, where ploughing has destroyed the later levels, the use of earth-shifting machinery involves changes in approach. The basic principles, however, remain unaltered. The development of geophysical methods of investigation has not been an unmixed advantage, for on some sites they may fail to detect buried features, thus giving a completely misleading idea of the distribution of occupation.

3

The Background

Hill-forts were being built and used in Britain for a thousand years or more, and were only one aspect, though an important one, of native life during that period. So although this is not a study of the Iron Age as a whole, some account of the chronology and cultural changes of that period is necessary as a background, as well as an indication of the nature of life then. What follows, though, is no more than a highly generalized outline.

As long ago as 1931 a coherent scheme of dated cultural changes was worked out by Professor Hawkes, and this, with some modifications and an extension by Professor Piggott to cover Scotland, held the field for nearly forty years. More recently, physical methods of dating have been developed, notably 'radiocarbon', depending on the proportions of radiocarbon which survive in organic remains, and 'thermoluminescence' which uses the property of minerals so that the age can be found by measuring variation of luminescence with temperature which is affected by the interval since the first heating. These methods have shown that almost all the dates deduced from the earlier scheme are much too late. This point is discussed in fuller detail below. In addition, some archaeologists believe that the detailed analysis of cultural characteristics depends too much on isolated elements, especially on pottery differences which now seem, in some cases at least, to correspond rather to the regions over which different groups of professional potters marketed their wares. Nevertheless, subject to the reservations over dating, this scheme provides the most useful basis for setting out, in broad outline, the development of the Iron Age.

The chronology presents the greatest problem. As already stated, radiocarbon determinations have demonstrated that many of the absolute dates suggested in the Hawkes-Piggott framework are a century or more too late: palisades for example, are there assigned to c. 450 BC, but recent radiocarbon figures indicate that some were in fact being built during the ninth century. Similarly, univallate hill-forts in Wales and the Marches are shown as starting rather after 250 BC, but the first rampart at Dinorben has given a radiocarbon date of 895 ± 95 BC. Indeed, the whole development of hill-forts before the Roman conquest has now to be spaced out over some nine or ten centuries, starting in the phase formally defined as the Late Bronze Age, and apparently at least as early in Scotland and Wales as in south-eastern England. According to the older scheme, a sixth-century date for a south-eastern fort was regarded as possible but daringly early, while all in the north and west were much later.

Despite these changes the Hawkes-Piggott scheme remains the only one consistently worked out to cover the whole of Britain, and the newer evidence does not, as yet, permit a complete new chronology. A framework recently proposed for the Welsh Marches is discussed below (p. 31). Further, most of the published material has used the older scheme as a background. It would be misleading arbitrarily to convert the dating assigned by an excavator to a supposedly more correct chronology, and the result could well be quite wrong. Equally, though, it would be misleading now to quote these dates as an absolute figure BC.

The method adopted, therefore, has been to quote the dates given by writers whose results are used, but to describe them as, for example, H 250, or second-century (H), when they appear to be based on the Hawkes-Piggott framework. This retains the carefully worked out relationships between sites in adjacent regions, which are often more important than absolute dates. It is impossible to give a conversion factor which will permit an accurate estimate of the 'true' BC date from 'H' figures, but *very* roughly they need to be multiplied by from $1\frac{1}{2}$ to $2\frac{1}{2}$ or even 3, the smaller values being applicable to the south-east, the larger to the north and west. It must be said, also, that the 'H' dates given here are sometimes inferred rather than directly quoted, and some of these inferences may be mistaken.

The other element of this scheme was the specification of the principal cultural characteristics of the British Iron Age; but probably its most important feature was the explicit recognition that culture and chronology must be treated separately. Thus the earliest cultural developments could have been entirely superseded and suppressed in one part of the country, while continuing to flourish elsewhere.

The principal characteristics of the British Iron Age can be recognized as the results of three main waves of continental influences, giving rise in this country to Iron Ages A, B and C. Their essentials are summarized below. They have now been subdivided, chronologically and geographically, so that a particular regional culture may be described, for example, as 'south-western second B', but for our purpose the simple basic classification is sufficient.

The first introduction of iron to this country seems to have been about H 600 or 700, but fully developed Iron Age A culture first appears about H 500, probably in the south and east, spreading slowly northwards and westwards to reach the remoter parts of Britain by H 300. It is characterized by pottery whose shape suggests derivation, usually at long remove, from metal bowls or buckets with carinated rims. Some of the better ware is given a red burnished coating of haematite as if to imitate bronze, but the nature of the coarser pots suggests that the population consisted mostly of descendants of the people who lived in Britain during the Late Bronze Age – a view confirmed by the survival of round houses as the predominant type, in contrast to the frequency of rectangular buildings on the continent. The hill-forts of this culture seem to have been exclusively defended by a single rampart, either a stone wall or a bank and ditch. Until recently, the first introduction of defended settlements to Britain was attributed to Iron Age A, and this probably remains true for their appearance in any numbers, but excavations at Ivinghoe Beacon have shown that the hill-fort there was associated exclusively with typically Late Bronze Age material; and radiocarbon dating has suggested a similarly early date on some other sites, notably Dinorben.

The second wave of foreign influences, Iron Age B, arrived in southern Britain about H 300 or 250, when 'A' had only just begun to replace the Late Bronze Age in the north and west. Their characteristic pottery takes the form of wide-mouthed rounded bowls. The ware is generally black or dark brown, often burnished, and the finer vessels are decorated with incised or simple stamped patterns, often with graceful curvilinear designs, especially in the later material. Much, if not all, of this pottery was produced commercially in particular districts, and distributed by trade. The new arrivals are credited with the introduction of the sling as a weapon, leading to the invention, perhaps in Britain, of defences consisting of two or more close-set banks and ditches. Again, the round house survives throughout much of Britain, indicating that these new arrivals also were a minority absorbed by or imposed on the mass of previous inhabitants. Nevertheless, along the whole of the Welsh Marches there seems to have been a settlement of groups entirely derived from abroad, indicated by the rows of square buildings as found at Croft Ambrey or Ffridd Faldwyn.

The third wave of continental influences, Iron Age C, arrived about H 100, introducing the use of coinage and of finer pottery, often wheel-turned. As settlers, they do not seem to have penetrated far outside south-eastern England. Settlements founded by them seem to have been protected by complex systems of linear earthworks, as at Colchester. They did occasionally take over existing hill-forts and improve and strengthen their defences. To judge from the evidence of Maiden Castle, moreover, they tidied up the settlements within the ramparts, sealing the stinking rubbish pits with layers of clean chalk or earth. The Belgae, whose invasion of Britain from north-east Gaul is recorded by Caesar, were the most noted among the bringers of this C culture.

The full-scale invasion by the Romans in AD 43 did not end the use of hill-forts immediately, but led to such a drastic discontinuity in their development that it is convenient to treat later events in a separate chapter.

As indicated earlier, the new evidence from radiocarbon dating has not yet been incorporated in a general chronological framework covering all Britain. An important beginning has been made in Scotland, but neither the structural sequences nor the artifacts there are as informative as those in the south. For the Welsh Marches, a comprehensive scheme covering nine centuries has been proposed by Mr S. C. Stanford, using the evidence of successive reconstructions in the gateways and other timberwork at Croft Ambrey and elsewhere and linking this to radiocarbon determinations.

The resulting chronology is likely to be much closer to the truth than the Hawkes-Piggott system, but cannot as yet be extended safely to other regions, such as the southern chalklands. Since the framework is based to a great extent on structural features, it is particularly useful in discussing their evolution (see p. 73), and it is of course directly applicable to the site of Croft Ambrey (pp. 99–101) which provided much of the information on which it is based. Nevertheless, the figures should still not be regarded as true dates BC, and are therefore referred to as 'S'. Thus stone guard chambers appear in the Marches about S 350.

The sparse documentary accounts which we have of Celtic life give the impression of a society dominated by priests (Druids) and warriors. No doubt this reflects their own estimate of their importance, but archaeologically they were no more than a thin layer of cream (or scum, according to one's social outlook) upon the great mass of people, who were essentially farmers. There was some trade, archaeologically attested in pottery as well as in utilitarian and fine metalwork, and to be inferred in livestock, but, except for the most skilled, craftsmen's markets were restricted to a radius of 30 or 40 kilometres from their base. So the population in any region, before the advent of the Romans and after their departure, would depend on the products of that region, not on imports. The sort of farming adopted was presumably that found by long experience to be most suited to the area. Generally in the south and east, and along the Welsh Marches, it seems to have been primarily arable, while in the extreme south-west, in Wales, and in the north, cattle predominated; but no area depended exclusively on a single product. It is also a fairly safe assumption that over most of the period the population would have increased to the limit imposed by the food supply. In general, then, as a rough upper approximation, the density of population may have been about the same as in the twelfth century AD; it is most unlikely to have been any greater. In the east and south, this implies something like ten to fifteen persons per square kilometre; the heavy claylands would not have been in use until just before the Roman period, so the medieval figure of twenty-five or so is likely to be too great. Elsewhere, the medieval value is probably of the right order, falling off to four to six per square kilometre in Wales, and to two or less in Scotland. In modern Britain population as sparse as this is only found near the remoter mountain districts. Even so, the mass of the population cannot have been reduced to bare subsistence. There was a surplus of production which could be creamed off for the benefit of the Druid priests, and to pay for the finely decorated metalwork of the warriors, or at least of their leaders. Time could be found, too, to build massive defences – and presumably to raid those of neighbours.

Even apart from the risk of death by violence, life was short. In Maiden Castle, for example, excluding the war cemetery, ages are known for skeletons from thirty-five bodies. Eleven of these died in infancy, nineteen below forty, four some time between forty and fifty, and one, the oldest, between forty-five and fifty-five. Those buried in the war cemetery, as might be expected, were on average younger, but included one man between fifty and sixty. Similar evidence is found elsewhere. Forty years, therefore, was the longest term one could reasonably hope for, even if one survived the dangers of childhood. This meagre life expectancy may be one reason for the extensive use of wood in structures which give the impression of intended permanence. A 30-centimetre oak beam would last for twenty years or more, so would only need to be renewed once in a man's working life.

So far as archaeological evidence goes, this brief span does not seem to have led to any great emphasis on existence after death. Cemeteries associated with hill-forts are extremely rare. Shrines have been identified in a few places, and may reasonably be inferred in others from temples of Roman date, which are fairly common, but little or nothing is known of the rituals with which they were served. What little is recorded concerning pre-Roman religious activities suggests that the main centres were located away from settlements.

4
Function

The really important part of a hill-fort was its interior. All too often, later use has obliterated any traces of the structures which stood there, so that most commonly nothing is known except the area enclosed and the arrangement of the protective ramparts. Nevertheless, even this limited information does allow some sort of classification: there is clearly a qualitative as well as a quantitative difference between enclosures of half a hectare and those fifty or a hundred times as large.

Excavation, and the evidence of visible hut emplacements where the ground has remained undisturbed, show that almost all hill-forts were inhabited. A few may have been intended as no more than temporary refuges, but the absence of relics or building traces does not necessarily prove this. Some cultures, for example, rely almost entirely on wooden or leather utensils, with no pottery; and certain types of building, such as timber houses founded on sleeper beams, may leave very little trace.

Whether the occupation of any fort was permanent or seasonal is a matter of inference. In southern Britain there would have been no practical objection to use throughout the year, for most of the sites are below 300 metres. The character of those excavated gives the impression that they were permanently inhabited. If the evidence from Tre'r Ceiri is correctly interpreted, this could apply even up to 500 metres. In Scotland, on the other hand, it seems incredible that places so far above sea level could have been occupied during the winter, so, making the reasonable assumption that the practice of transhumance goes back to prehistoric times, these high-level hill-forts could have been used for protection when the herds were moved up to the summer pastures.

Lacking excavation, size is probably the most important clue to a hill-fort's function, but it is important to realize that although modern terms have to be used in such a discussion they are at best no more than a rough approximation to the reality. Just as the military associations of the term 'fort' give a misleading idea of the true nature of one of these places, so the words 'city', 'town', 'castle' and even 'village' or 'farm' carry with them ideas which are often not appropriate to early settlements. In particular, practically nothing can be known or even guessed as to their administrative organization; even where some fairly early documentary material survives and should apparently be relevant, only the most brutally Procrustean treatment of the archaeological facts can make the details appear to fit. In what follows, these reservations must be kept in mind.

A second generalization, to which also there may be some exceptions, especially among the largest enclosures, is that the inhabitants of most British hill-forts subsisted on the produce of their immediate neighbourhood. Apart from some of the largest coastal forts, there is no reason to suppose that any substantial part of the population depended primarily on trade. This does not, of course, preclude the occurrence of seasonal 'fairs' for the exchange of produce, especially in cattle-raising areas.

Most hill-forts are simple enclosures, more or less strongly protected, the lines of defence being adapted to the form of the ground. In some regions, especially the south-west (pp. 44–5) and the Scottish borders (p. 45), subsidiary enclosures can be interpreted as intended for the protection of flocks and herds, but more often the appearance of multiple compartments is the result of successive alterations and reconstructions, so that the structure remained functionally one enclosure, the additional banks falling into disuse as at Maiden Castle and Hambledon Hill. Rarely, they may have continued in use as an extra defence, as perhaps at Pen Dinas, Aberystwyth.

The nature of the smallest enclosures is fairly certain. These would mostly correspond to the homes of single families, some of the larger including servants or slaves. The more weakly defended can be compared to the moated farms of the Middle Ages. Examples can be picked almost at random throughout Britain, but are under-represented in the gazetteer, which has concentrated on more impressive works. Nevertheless, Am Baghan Burblach, the northern enclosure on Harding's Down, Little Woodbury and Staple Howe are of this kind.

Considering Britain as a whole, these small weakly protected enclosures are numerically the commonest type of 'hill-fort', but many others, equally small internally and thus likely to be homes of a single family, have defences which now look disproportionately strong, often covering a greater area than that enclosed. The Barmekin of Echt, Chun Castle, the various Castle Laws, Dunsinane and Honington may be mentioned. For such places, the analogy with a medieval castle may be apt, since the task of construction seems too great to be the work of the occupants alone, and this implies that they were able to call in others to help.

There is no precise limit at which single family establishments give way to 'villages', but in some districts, such as south-west Wales, there is a break in the sequence of sizes, or a change in the distribution pattern, near 0·7 hectare, which suggests that the transition may occur at about that area; this is no more than a general trend, and does not as yet justify abandoning the 1·2 hectare criterion used by the Ordnance Survey. The larger enclosures can be regarded as 'villages' or 'towns'. Where the dividing line should be drawn is a matter of definition, and discussion would be unprofitable until far more work has been done on regional size distribution.

There are a few enclosures which stand out as quite exceptional, such as Llanymynech (56 hectares) or Bindon Hill (114 hectares). Even assuming no more than thirty persons per hectare, places of this size would need to draw on an improbably large district to maintain their inhabitants, so they must either have been far less densely occupied than the normal hill-fort or must have depended for their subsistence on something more than the farm produce of the adjacent countryside. No single explanation will fit all the examples. Bindon Hill has been accounted for as an invasion base, but an equally satisfactory alternative would be to regard it as a trading centre. This latter function would certainly seem appropriate for Hengistbury Head, also unusually large, where there is a fair amount of evidence of foreign contacts. Llanymynech, on the other hand, lies well inland, and seems most easily explicable as a centre for occasional assemblies by the local tribe, the Cornovii. Each of these very large enclosures needs to be considered separately, in its local context.

5

Distribution and Regional Types

Hill-forts are a characteristic feature of Iron Age culture, but it is immediately obvious from the maps (figs 1–3) that they are not an essential one. These maps require some explanation.

To give a really adequate cartographic representation of the distribution of hill-forts is not practicable, for it would require an atlas of several sheets, all at a very much larger scale. All that has been attempted, therefore, is to represent the size distribution, since area is probably the most important single quality. Even so, to avoid the excessive multiplication of different symbols, it has been necessary to use each to cover a wide range of areas. For consistency, the Ordnance Survey Iron Age map limits of 1·2 and 6 hectares have been adopted, but have been supplemented by two further critical values, 0·24 hectare to define the very small enclosures and 30 hectares to separate out those which are very large. These are not necessarily the best figures to choose, apart from the fact that the separate classes cover such a wide range of size; but further research is needed before more significant criteria can be selected. In the northern map the little fortified enclosures known as 'duns' have been shown, since there is no clear dividing line between a dun and a very small hill-fort; their distribution has been taken from the map which accompanies the work on the *Iron Age in Northern Britain*. Generally the objective has been to show every known fort, but in some very crowded areas, such as the Scottish borders, a few of the smallest have had to be omitted.

In considering the significance of the pattern shown by these maps, it is important to realize that it represents a palimpsest, built up over some thousand years. Nevertheless, since the dates of the various forts can seldom be decided, the distribution has to be considered as a whole. Some features stand out immediately. South of Hadrian's Wall about 1,420 hill-forts are known, and all but 110 of these lie south-west of a line from the Dee to Dungeness. Again, in the north

KEY (within figure):

△ MULTIVALLATE, SOUTH-WESTERN TYPE
● OVER 30 HECTARES
◯ OVER 6 TO 30 HECTARES
○ OVER 1.2 TO 6 HECTARES
○ OVER 0.24 TO 1.2 HECTARES
• 0.24 HECTARE & UNDER

Fig. 1 Hill-forts in south-west Britain. Based upon the Ordnance Survey Map with the sanction of the Controller of Her Majesty's Stationary Office, Crown copyright reserved.

of Britain, there are 1,100 or so (if duns are rejected), and of these a third lie between the wall and a line joining north Berwick to Portpatrick. These contrasts cannot be explained simply in geographical terms, as for example by variations in the fertility of the soil, but must reflect some social differences.

The lack of uniformity in distribution becomes even more striking if size is taken into account. Several major regions can be recognized.

In most of the west and south of Wales, and in Cornwall and most of Devon, the forts are predominantly small and very numerous. Further east, in a triangle with its base extending from the Exe to Southampton Water, and its vertex just west of the Dee, large forts are common, but with a considerable admixture of smaller ones. Then up to the Dee-Dungeness line, the forts are almost all large, and appreciably less frequent. Finally, so far as the rest of Britain south of Hadrian's Wall in concerned, hill-forts become rare.

In the north there is a similar diversity. The heavy concentration in the Scottish Border region has already been mentioned. These are generally small enclosures, as indeed are most of those in the north. Then there is a fairly dense scatter round the firths of the Forth and Tay, followed by a sparse distribution of medium-sized enclosures up the east coast, while on the west coast hill-forts become rare. In the south, their infrequency is counterbalanced by the great mass of duns.

Thus there are at least seven or eight distinct regions, recognizably different though their boundaries are not sharp. These regions, moreover, arc distinguishable using very broad criteria, and there is no doubt that really careful and detailed investigation would make further subdivision possible. It must be added that although regional types of fort, where identifiable, may well have corresponded to a particular tribe, this is a hypothesis which can neither be proved nor disproved; for tribal locations are seldom known before the Roman period, and their boundaries usually have an uncertainty of 30 or 40 kilometres at least. In most cases, also, the territory to be associated with a hill-fort must remain uncertain; but J. F. Dyer has put forward convincing arguments for accepting certain dykes in the eastern Chilterns as being Iron Age territorial boundaries. For the South Downs, the discussions by B. Cunliffe and R. Bradley (see p. 104) suggest the probable general areas controlled by the inhabitants of some hill-forts. Conversely, the absence of any obvious boundaries which might limit the regions appertaining to forts such as

MULTIVALLATE, SOUTH-WESTERN TYPE
△ MULTIVALLATE, SOUTH-WESTERN TYPE
● OVER 30 HECTARES
◯ OVER 6 TO 30 HECTARES
○ OVER 1.2 TO 6 HECTARES
○ OVER 0.24 TO 1.2 HECTARES
· 0.24 HECTARE & UNDER

Bigberry, Clare or Tasburgh gives some support to the idea that these places may have been in a sense political 'capitals'.

In the case of Bigberry, this identification is supported by the establishment of Canterbury nearby as the Roman cantonal capital — Durovernum Cantiacorum. There are similar associations of hill-forts with cantonal capitals elsewhere, as Llanmelin with Caerwent, (Venta Silurum) or St Catherine's Hill with Winchester (Venta Belgarum). But the argument is not irrefutable, for neither Llanmelin nor St Catherine's Hill is an exceptionally impressive hill-fort, and the latter seems likely to have been abandoned well before the Roman invasion.

In these eastern regions, the presence of a few isolated forts, and by implication a considerable number of undefended settlements also, must imply a fairly well organized social system, in which some centralized control prevented casual raiding by neighbours. The normally peaceful character of these regions is emphasized by the developments which took place at Stanwick in Yorkshire. There, a fairly small hill-fort of normal type, in a region where they are not common, became the nucleus of a great system of enclosures fortified by dykes, resembling the Belgic *oppida* of the south-east. All this has been convincingly interpreted as the capital of Venutius, where he collected his troops and his allies in preparation for his revolt after AD 50.

In contrast, the extreme south-west and west, and the Scottish borders, display intense concentrations of small enclosures, though a few larger ones exist there as well.

Enough of these small sites have been examined in south-west Wales to demonstrate that they are not all of the same type, nor probably of the same date, and so far as can be judged at present from surface evidence they range with no obvious break from structures to which only the most extreme purist would deny the description 'hill-fort' down to lightly protected enclosures on almost level ground. Some of these last, as at Trelissey, have proved to contain a small Roman house, which may have been the successor of a native farm. On the other hand, at Walesland Rath full excavation of what appeared on the surface to be a comparable structure has revealed a

Fig. 2 Hill-forts in south-east Britain. Based upon the Ordnance Survey Map with the sanction of the Controller of Her Majesty's Stationery Office, Crown copyright reserved.

Fig. 3   Hill-forts in northern Britain. Based upon the Ordnance Survey Map with the sanction of the Controller of Her Majesty's Stationery Office, Crown copyright reserved.

two-period settlement of great complexity, with rows of rectangular buildings following the inner circuit of the rampart, and six or eight round houses in the central space. It can be explained with equal plausibility as anything from a dependent village to the 'court' of a local 'lord', with various other alternatives. The investigation has thus a double importance, both as one of the rare examples of full scientific excavation and as a warning against too facile interpretation of incomplete data.

Nevertheless, though questions of detail remain unanswered, these regions with numerous small defended enclosures must imply the existence of a very different social organization from that found further east. Perhaps a fairly close modern parallel would be the background to life on both sides of the Scottish borders in the sixteenth century. Raiding would normally be against people at a distance, but local quarrels could spark off an attack on an immediate neighbour. Keeping in mind that no analogy can be exact, we may note the range from strongly defended enclosures with several ramparts, through weaker settlements with single banks such as Walesland, to places which now appear barely defensible, and compare it to the impressive pele towers of the rich landowner, the 'bastle houses', and the peles themselves, simple enclosures without towers, which have now mostly vanished. Straining the parallel still further, we may even suspect that some of the rare larger hill-forts were the dwellings of rulers having some nominal regional authority, rather more localized than that of some English and Scottish royalty early in the Middle Ages, but equally ineffective.

In regions of intermediate type, where hill-forts are fairly large but also fairly numerous, much more detailed analysis of their distribution is needed: the apparent similarity of the pattern over a large area may conceal regional differences. In west Caernarvonshire, for example, it is possible to determine approximately the territory which might be associated with the two large forts of Garn Boduan and Carn Fadrun, and at a rough estimate this could have supported some thousand to fifteen hundred people, approximately the total population of those two hill-forts. It is therefore possible, though not of course certain, that these were the only substantial inhabited places in that region.

By contrast, if the hill-forts of west Kent, west Sussex, Surrey and the adjacent parts of Hampshire are examined similarly, it appears that they have relatively much larger areas associated with them.

They were therefore either very much more crowded than forts in similar territory further west (such as Hod Hill, where the surviving hut emplacements permit an estimate of population), or they each formed some sort of social or commercial centre for a population of which half or more normally lived at some distance. Once again using a dangerous analogy, they would be comparable to a medieval market town. Unlike the hill-forts of east Kent or East Anglia, there is no need to suppose that any part of their dependent territory lay more than 15 or 20 kilometres distant.

These settlements on the southern chalklands have received fuller attention than those elsewhere. The excavations at Quarley Hill demonstrated the relationship of that enclosure to earlier dykes, or ranch boundaries of the late Bronze Age. Professor Cunliffe and R. Bradley have emphasized the significant associations of settlements with features likely to be connected with cattle-raising and often with sacred places (inferred from the later erection of Roman temples). Many of the major hill-forts of this region can therefore be convincingly interpreted as having developed out of traditional meeting places which combined the functions of seasonal fairs or markets and those of religious centres. It is easy to devise hypotheses which will explain the evolution leading from groups of herdsmen ranging over open downland to the construction of large fortified villages, each centred on a traditional nucleus and under the control of some local leader, perhaps loosely subject to a tribal ruler.

When structural characteristics and details of design are taken into account as well as enclosed area, various regional groups can be recognized. The best known of these is characteristic of south-western Britain, the south-western wide-spaced multivallate hill-fort, to give its full description; its special characteristics were first recognized by Lady Fox. Milber Down and Clovelly Dykes are type sites. A relatively small main enclosure, seldom as much as a hectare in area and usually univallate, is surrounded by one or more additional slighter ramparts, each separated from the enclosures by wide spaces. This arrangement is convincingly interpreted as designed for the protection of cattle, the innermost small enclosure being the actual homestead. Almost all known examples occur in the south-west, and seem to be associated with B culture, dating from H 200 or later. There are several variants of the plan, the differences being mainly in the arrangement of the outer enclosures, which are not always symmetrically placed relative to the 'homestead'; but all follow the same basic principle of a small enclosure with slighter outworks widely spaced.

A few of the forts on the Scottish borders seem to have some provision for cattle. The Ringses on Doddington Moor has a compartment between inner and outer defences, with a separate entrance; but the outer rampart is stronger than in the normal 'south-western' type, and the enclosed space much smaller. At Lordenshaws the outer dyke may be a rather closer parallel. These two little forts, apart from this possible provision for cattle, may represent a 'type' which extends fairly widely into southern Scotland, characterized by strong defences enclosing a small more or less oval space, as also at Bochastle and Dunsinane, among others; but whether all these really deserve to be regarded as a single type is open to question.

At one time the 'vitrified forts' of Scotland were looked upon as a separate class, but these are now recognized as merely sharing a widespread use of timber reinforcement. Nevertheless, they do seem to include a group of characteristic and distinctive plan, though with a wide range of areas, as at Castle Law, Forgandenny, Finavon, Barry Hill near Perth and the White Caterthun. All those are more or less oblong with semicircular ends, and the type seems to have a rather localized scatter on both sides of the Firth of Tay.

Another type which seems to be exclusively Scottish, and to be post-Roman, is the nuclear fort, exemplified particularly by Dundurn, Dunadd and Ruberslaw. These have been built on craggy sites which form small irregular shelves. Each shelf is separately walled, so that the highest 'citadel' is approached through a series of defended courts, each commanded by the one above. Unfortunately no really characteristic fort of this kind has been scientifically excavated, and the possibility cannot be excluded that the apparent 'nuclear' arrangement may be the result of successive alterations and additions to what was originally a simple enclosure. That is certainly the case with some forts claimed to be of this type, but the three named at least give a strong impression of unitary design.

There are other features which seem to have a localized distribution, but which have not yet been studied fully enough for their extent to be known. One of the most important and interesting is the use of small rectangular buildings, as at Croft Ambrey; this practice seems to follow, roughly, a broad belt of territory along the Welsh Marches. Another distinctive characteristic is the use of paired guard chambers, found at Croft Ambrey but also at Dinorben (where the dwellings were round), and probably at Maiden Castle, as well as at Rainsborough, though there the chambers were round not rectangular. Massive multiple defences with elaborate entrances, as at Maiden Castle, also seem to be limited to the same general area. Nevertheless, the distributions of these three features are certainly not coincident, and multivallation is common in the Scottish borders also, though not much further north.

On the other hand, some technical devices occur in widely separated isolated patches. The *chevaux-de-frise* is discussed below (pp. 48–9). The use of large upright slabs to line entrance passages, as at Garrywhin and Duchary Rock, occurs in a fairly restricted area of north-east Scotland, but is found also at Conway Mountain and elsewhere in Wales. Multiple small entrances are also found in both these regions: they exist at Duchary Rock, and at Tre'r Ceiri. To what extent characteristics of this kind are significant is something which can only be determined when far more of our hill-forts have been the subjects of really detailed and accurate surveys. There is no doubt that when that has been done still more regional types will become recognizable.

6

Origins, Attack and Defence

Until recently, the first use of iron in Britain and the appearance of hill-forts were accepted as roughly contemporary and as having been introduced by invaders from the continent about H 500. Excavations, notably at Ivinghoe Beacon and Dinorben, but confirmed at some other sites, have now shown that some defences must have been put up within the period formally assigned to the Late Bronze Age, well before the earliest traces of ironworking here; in true dates, these sites may well go back as far as 900 or 1000 BC. Although this does not necessarily rule out the invasion hypothesis, it falsifies the dramatic picture of hordes of warriors, armed with better (and cheaper) weapons of iron, setting up fortified invasion bases on the British coasts. Once again, any sort of unitary explanation is likely to be misleading.

Walls, field banks or fences, much like those seen at many farms today, were built during the Bronze Age. To enlarge these to form a defensive rampart would require no particular inventive powers, so all that would be needed to give rise to a hill-fort would be some stimulus which would make the work seem worthwhile. Several such can be imagined, but the simplest would be merely an increase in population, especially if combined with settled farming methods, which could themselves lead to such an increase. The defences could either be the work of the original inhabitants, or could have been built by aggressors moving into new territory. Once the 'hill-fort idea' was established, also, the mere possession of defences might have carried with it some prestige.

Hill-forts, therefore, can be expected to appear as a purely local phenomenon, independently of any external influences; but that is not to say that they always did so. When technical details characteristic of forts in central Europe are found almost unchanged in Sussex, for example, the movement of ideas, and probably of actual people, can reasonably be assumed (see also pp. 61–3, 204, 274). Fortifications in central Europe provide exact parallels to the panels of dry-stone walling between timber uprights, as at Maiden Castle for example, and to an even more distinctive arrangement where the uprights, with or without stone walling, are tied together by horizontal timbers running from back to front of the rampart; Preist, in Bavaria, is the type site. This needs to be distinguished from the true *murus gallicus* described by Caesar, which is not found in Britain. Preist-type reinforcement, or arrangements very similar, occurs widely in Britain, and in some very early contexts, as at Dinorben. Bindon Hill, above Lulworth Cove, may have been an actual invasion base for people building in this style.

Technical tricks found in stone ramparts also occur abroad, but are less certainly of foreign origin. The use of multiple facing, believed to be the *murus duplex* of Caesar, is common throughout France and in Britain, as also are ramparts stepped at the back, but both techniques seem so obvious that they could have been invented independently. Double facing, presumably to reduce the risk of collapse, is found in neolithic and Bronze Age burial cairns.

Ditch profiles have not been much studied; but the use of a very broad flat-bottomed ditch in front of a massive single rampart seems characteristic of some French fortifications, mostly in the north: it is known as the Fécamp type from the site where it was first identified. It is also found at Oldbury in Kent and probably at East Hill, Hastings, among others in south-east England. It may have been developed in response to Roman methods of attack.

All these have a fairly continuous distribution, and there is no difficulty in envisaging ways in which the techniques could have been carried from place to place. One very distinctive type of additional defence, however, presents a great problem. That is the *chevaux-de-frise*, where a broad band in front of the rampart is set with a close-set pattern of small pointed stones. The known distribution in western Europe seems to be restricted to central Spain and Britain, with no intervening examples; and the British examples are sporadic, two or three in Wales, and a few in Scotland and Ireland. At one of the Welsh sites, Pen-y-Gaer near Llanbedr-y-Cennin, the belt of pointed stones is bounded on its outer edge by a slight bank and ditch, reproducing an arrangement identical with one which occurs in Spain. Possible explanations for this peculiar distribution are that of independent invention; that there is a wide spread of timber examples, all undiscovered, linking the known distributions of those in stone; or that small bodies of refugees from central Spain settled independently in various parts of Britain (but without opposition, for most of the examples are inland). None of these is satisfactory, and the problem remains unsolved.

Some element of display may often have been present in hill-fort design. For example, the panels of white stonework between the dark timber uprights at Maiden Castle must have been architecturally quite impressive until the timber rotted. Nevertheless, the primary object was to resist attack. Even if traditions which imply chariot warfare in the open were universally applicable, they would not conflict with this view, for ideally a fortress should be so strong as to make any thought of attack appear hopeless. It follows that if *both* sides wished to meet in battle, such a meeting, with or without chariots, would take place outside the ramparts. An actual assault either implies a surprise raid or an apparent numerical advantage by the attackers.

Archaeological evidence for such attacks, except at the time of the Roman invasions, is necessarily rare and seldom completely unambiguous. Those who adhere to the theory that all Iron Age warfare was in the open can explain away evidence for defenders killed in battle as a massacre of non-combatants after defeat; and any burned gateway can be written off either as due to the same circumstances or as pure accident. Nevertheless, to do this in all cases seems to be straining the evidence to fit a preconceived theory. At Sutton Walls, the skeletons showing marks of weapons and casually thrown into the ditches seem likely to be those of the young men who fell during the capture of the fortress. Similarly, at Bredon Hill the remains of bodies which had been literally cut to pieces were found scattered over the gate passage. Fragments from a handsome shield were found buried under a fallen wall at Moel Hiraddug. And while some fires were no doubt accidental, the excavator's interpretation of the burning of the first gateway at Rainsborough as the result of attack is convincing. Evidence of this kind requires that the attack ended the occupation. Even though the people of the period do not seem to have been unduly fastidious, they would surely have tidied away most of the bodies and generally have repaired the defences if the place remained inhabited.

At the time of the Roman conquest, there can be no doubt that some of the larger settlements put up a defence. It is only necessary to cite the example of Hod Hill, where additional ramparts were under construction when the place fell, and where the excavator traced the pattern of ballista bolts aimed at one of the principal dwellings. At Maiden Castle, too, even if the warriors buried in the war cemetery did not die within the town, as seems likely, the Romans considered it worthwhile to slight the gateway, making it militarily useless; clearly they regarded the ramparts as intended for defence, not merely for show.

Almost the only written account of native warfare is that given by Caesar in his *Gallic Wars*, when the influence of Roman methods had begun to be felt. The simplest method was to drive the defenders off the ramparts by a shower of missiles; the attackers, with shields above their heads, then undermined the wall and set fire to the gates. Was it perhaps in a battle of this kind that the Moel Hiraddug shield was lost?

Any form of dry-stone construction would be vulnerable to this sort of attack, though the steep slope of rubble from the collapsed wall would still be a fairly effective obstacle to the assailants. Rather surprisingly, there is no mention of the use of scaling ladders by the Gauls. Not only gateways, but in dry weather even timber revetments, could be destroyed by fire, and Caesar describes an attack on a Roman camp, using incendiary darts and red-hot slingstones of baked clay.

Perhaps the most instructive incident in Caesar's account is the siege of Uxellodunum (Puy d' Issolu, near Vayrac – *pace* the rival claimants). This is an immense plateau the size of the City of London, nearly impregnable owing to its surrounding cliffs. Yet the inhabitants depended almost entirely on water fetched from the river Dordogne far below, or from a sacred spring, nearer but still outside the defences. Unknown to the defenders, Caesar tapped its source by an adit, and this apparently supernatural blow reduced them to such despair that they surrendered.

It is evident from this account that the occupants of even a large and well organized town felt no need for a supply of water within the walls, but were prepared to bring most of their requirements from a considerable distance. The absence of any wells or cisterns in most British forts indicates that the same practice prevailed here. It also supports the view that the defences were for protection from casual raids, rather than against deliberately planned assaults in the course of systematic warfare.

In Britain, the documentary record of the Roman conquest,

confirmed by excavation, indicates that even massive fortresses such as Maiden Castle and Hod Hill fell quickly to the invaders' disciplined persistence and superior siege engines, but so far only the latter site has produced evidence of the actual methods used. There Sir Ian Richmond worked out the distribution of ballista bolts round and in one of the principal dwellings, and was able to infer the approximate position of the engine from which these came. No example has been recognized, in this country, of the method of attack by constructing a massive bank rising to the level of the ramparts; this would leave traces which should be still visible, and some may await identification.

Defence can be considered in its active and passive forms. There was one great development in the method of active defence, the introduction of the sling as a weapon, perhaps about H 200 or H 300 in this country. More precisely, of course, the same weapons are available for attack or for defence; but, as will be seen below, the sling, combined with appropriate rampart design, gave a decisive advantage to the defenders, other things being equal.

Before the introduction of sling warfare, the normal function of a rampart was to provide an elevated platform for defence, difficult for the attackers to climb, and with some frontal protection for the defenders. There was no great advantage in keeping the enemy at a distance. The ideal was to get them trapped in a ditch immediately below the rampart, so that they were vulnerable to short-range missiles, and to the spears or swords of the defenders if they did manage to get within reach. Very rarely, a *chevaux-de-frise* was provided outside the ditch, to break up a charge. Forts built before the widespread adoption of the sling as a weapon should therefore tend to have a single rampart, with a ditch where the ground permits, and with a breastwork along the outer side of the rampart walk.

The sling changed the whole principle of defence. A sling stone travels approximately in a parabola, so increased height gives greatly increased range. The ideal defensive profile therefore has a high main rampart, with two or more lesser ramparts in front, each having a steep but sloping outer face so as to give the attacker no cover, and an almost vertical back to prevent retreat. The rampart top needs no frontal breastwork, for it would hinder the use of the sling; any fence which there is will, in an ideal design, be along the back of the rampart walk as at Maiden Castle. To increase the firepower beyond what would be possible using only the top of the bank; platforms may be provided at lower levels, though no really convincing examples are known in Britain. Forts were not always built in the most up-to-date style, or exactly as this theory would suggest; indeed, sling stone hoards are found in some univallate forts. But most of the impressive monumental multivallate enclosures can be attributed to the introduction of the new weapon. It has been suggested that the use of multiple ramparts was invented in Britain as a response to this.

The most vulnerable part of the defences was the entrance. Apart from a simple gate or hurdle, the commonest elaboration was the provision of a bridge, and arrangement of the approach so that a direct rush was impossible and any attackers could be overlooked from a length of rampart. Some of the complexities which resulted are described later (chapter 9).

It is impossible to generalize about the fate of the inhabitants after an unsuccessful defence. In Caesar's wars, this varied according to circumstances from collection of tribute and hostages to execution of the leaders and mutilation of all fighting men, or to the sale of the whole tribe as slaves. Examples of destruction and massacre have been mentioned earlier, and most of these may well have been the results of native warfare. The Romans could be equally barbarous, but there are enough examples where occupation continued into the Roman period to suggest that their usual policy was to allow the inhabitants to remain, probably with their defences slighted, until they chose of their own accord to move to a more Romanized type of settlement.

7

Building the Hill-Fort

The immediate reasons for building a hill-fort, or for choosing a particular site, can usually only be guessed at. The south chalklands are exceptional in that a convincing theory has been put forward to account for the positions of the forts (p. 44), but even there the immediate stimulus which led to the construction of the actual defences remains uncertain. Claims have often been made that forts form deliberately planned strategic systems, but these hypotheses are not necessary to account for the distributions of the sites. Similarly, at the beginning of this century, several writers made a great point of the intervisibility of hill-forts; but hill tops can usually be seen from other hill tops, and it has never been demonstrated that the number of fortified sites visible one from another is greater than would occur by chance. Another theory put forward is that the exploitation of lead may have dictated the location of hill-forts in north Cardiganshire; but the region is so rich in ore that it would be difficult to find a hill which was not fairly near a vein. There are ways in which these ideas could be tested, but until that has been done they must be dismissed as unproven speculations. Even if they should prove to be true, they would not necessarily imply that the location of forts was subject to some centralized control.

There seems, in fact, to be no need to suppose that the decision to build a hill-fort, its choice of site or its form of construction, was the concern of anyone other than the group who built it, though of course they would be influenced by fashion and by the imminence of danger. Usually, too, the position chosen seems to have been that which could be effectively defended with the least work. Where this is not the case, many explanations can be imagined, ranging from a practical need to fortify a pre-existing settlement to supernatural guidance; the curious events at Dinas Emrys may have been a survival of the sort of thing which was formerly normal. Evidence, inevitably, is lacking.

For the actual details of construction there is much information available, especially from unfinished work. This has recently been studied very fully by Dr R. W. Feachem; the classic site is Ladle Hill in Hampshire, described by Professor Piggott in 1931. Despite the many examples discovered subsequently, this remains the one where the evidence is clearest. The organization of the work was perhaps rather exceptionally systematic and well planned.

The design envisaged was a roughly circular enclosure, protected by a single rampart built up of material from an external ditch. The plan was first marked out on the ground by a small bank and ditch. Material from the excavation of the main ditch was then transported to dumps within the enclosure. It may be assumed that the disadvantage of double-handling was acceptable, partly to allow the material to be sorted so that the larger chalk could be used at the base of the rampart, and partly because it was to be built up behind a timber revetment. Some parts of the rampart had been completed, when the work of fortification was given up, either because the danger was past or because the enemy arrived too soon. It seems clear that the workers were divided into gangs some of which worked faster than others, but the whole scheme must have been supervised by a single director.

Although some sort of marking out is usual, not all the unfinished enclosures show evidence of such efficient organization. Work at the easternmost fort of the group on Harding's Down in Gower stands at the other extreme. Here, the original design was for a typical 'south-western' fort, with a fairly strong inner enclosure separated by a wide space from an outer bank. The latter was of no great strength, and seems to have been completed, but only half the inner enclosure was built; work on it must have been very haphazard.

There is no sign of a marking out ditch, so presumably the circuit was indicated by a few upright sticks. The east half of the rampart, including the entrance, seems to have been finished, with a massive stone revetment (now removed) at the rear. At the western end, also, a short length was built up to its full height. These two parts, however, are unconnected, so although a lot of work has been done the place is quite indefensible. Evidently the work was divided up among gangs, some of whom did nothing at all, and such overall control as there was could neither enforce the general decision on the inactive gangs nor arrange for the others to provide a slight rampart round the whole circuit rather than bring their own sections to full completion. To assign sections to separate gangs seems to have been the normal way in which work on ramparts was organized, for there are many examples of unfinished ditches or of ramparts only brought to their full height in places; but the work has usually been carried far enough to provide some sort of defence.

In both these examples, material for the ramparts was obtained from an exterior ditch which formed part of the defences, but hill-fort builders were not doctrinaire about this. Their objective was simply to provide a strong fortification, and on a steep hillside this could often be done more easily by building up the main rampart from quarries behind it, the material from the ditch being also thrown downhill to form a counterscarp bank. The inner quarry ditches usually provided sheltered level places for dwellings; the stratified filling which accumulated is one of the major sources of information for the excavator.

The local or national worthy laying a foundation deposit is an innocuous survival of a very ancient tradition. The earliest account of such a ceremony in Britain occurs in the story concerning Dinas Emrys. There is no way of telling whether the magical elements have been superimposed on a genuine tradition or whether the whole tale is fiction, but even in this post-Roman context the storyteller gives no hint that there was anything unusual in the idea that Druids might advise a human sacrifice in order to ensure stability for a fortress. Certainly the practice is attested much earlier at both Maiden Castle and Hod Hill. Further skeletons have also been found from bodies apparently casually deposited in the ramparts at the former site and at South Cadbury, among other places. These are usually regarded as members of the workforce who died during construction, but were more probably sacrificial deposits, for considering the care generally employed in building the ramparts it seems unlikely that the supervisor would accept such very unsuitable material unless its structural weakness were counterbalanced by the advantage of spiritual support. The number of possible examples remains very small; but proportionately to the total length of Iron Age ramparts in Britain the amount which has been completely excavated to the original surface is infinitesimal. Moreover, simpler ceremonies such as libations would leave no trace.

The setting out being completed, and any necessary ceremonies performed, work could start. The great multiple ramparts of places such as Maiden Castle or Hod Hill suggest that decades of toil are represented, and in a sense that is true; but these huge defences did not reach their present state in a single step.

Fortunately, work on the experimental earthwork at Overton Down has given an indication of the rate at which a ditch could be dug in chalk: it works out at about 1 to 1·3 cubic metres per man, per day, to loosen the material, dig it out and transport it to a bank. The tools used were picks made of deer antler, shoulderblades of oxen for shovels and baskets for transport.

Applying these figures to the projected rampart at Ladle Hill: this measured 680 metres in length, and may be assumed for this calculation to have been, in intent, 4 metres high, 7 metres wide at the base and 1 metre at the summit, giving a total volume of just under 11,000 cubic metres, requiring between 8,000 and 11,000 man-days' work. To allow for the double-handling involved on this site, this time must be increased by half: the rock did not need to be loosened before the second transference. Also, about 1,000 small trees would be needed for the timberwork. No experiments on cutting these have been published, but 500 man-days would seem reasonable for that part of the work. These add up to a total of about 12,500 to 17,000 man-days. Making the conservative assumption of 60 persons per hectare in this fort of 3·4 hectares, about 200 people would give a work-force equivalent to perhaps 150 men, for women and children would help as basket-carriers. So a total of about 85 to 115 days would be sufficient to complete a hill-fort of this kind. It must be obvious that these figures are merely an indication of possibility. They probably err rather on the high side, for one may suppose that a rather larger population would hope to benefit from the protection of the fort, and would thus assist in building it.

The rampart projected at Ladle Hill was not exceptional; huge defences such as those at Maiden Castle remain awe-inspiring. Excavation there, though, has shown that they reached their present form in several stages. There is no need to give the calculations in full, but making the same assumptions for density of population and rate of work as for Ladle Hill, the following results are obtained. The first rampart, enclosing the eastern knoll, would have taken 100 to 150 days (assuming double-handling); the extension to form the first enlarged enclosure only needed 25 to 30 days, for the population was presumably larger, much of the old rampart could be incorporated, and the glacis-type construction would not involve double-handling. Both subsequent alterations would, by contrast, have required something of the order of 150 to 250 days, perhaps needing to be spread out over two or three years. In fact, the occupants of Maiden Castle must almost certainly have been able to call upon helpers from surrounding territory; and even if they could not, these final stages were improvements to works which were already fully defensible.

The large hill-forts, then, offer no great problem. Places enclosing about 3 or 4 hectares or more, with an assumed population of sixty persons per hectare, could have been made defensible in two to four months. It is the smaller enclosures, presumed single family farms, which present difficulty. For a place a quarter the area of Ladle Hill, and thus theoretically with a quarter the population, the volume of rampart material will only be halved; so it would take at least 170 days to build, too great a proportion of the year for people who have to grow their own food. In such a case, possible explanations are a higher density of occupation, assistance from outside, or work spread over several years. The same explanation need not be applicable to every fort. As yet, excavators do not seem to have directed their attention to the difficult question of whether a single phase of rampart-building was completed in one season or spread over two or three years.

Not every small hill-fort has such massive ramparts, and many could be made defensible in a reasonable time. Take as a final example the fairly typical Camp Tops at Morebattle in Roxburghshire, where the eight dwellings of the occupants can still be traced, implying a population of about forty, equivalent to a work-force of thirty. A fairly accurate estimate can be made of the volume of material in each rampart: inner, 900 cubic metres, requiring 22 to 30 days' work; middle 570, 14 to 19 days; and outer 360, 9 to 12 days. So the inner rampart, making the site defensible, could have been finished within a month, and the whole structure in two.

8

The Ramparts

The materials available to hill-fort builders were earth, stone and timber, and these were combined in almost every imaginable conjunction. Turf was seldom used. It served as filling at Carlwark and Rainsborough, but in general its rarity contrasts strongly with its very frequent employment by the Romans in semi-permanent works. Caesar notes that his enemies in northern Gaul had learned the use of turf for rampart-building from prisoners, but had no proper tools for the work and had to use their swords to cut it. Iron was used very sparingly indeed in construction in pre-Roman Britain; even at gateways it is uncommon. Mortared masonry is invariably Roman or later.

Many of the techniques were used two millennia earlier by the builders of neolithic tombs, but are not demonstrable in the intervening period, so for most of them re-introduction or re-invention must be postulated. Not enough is known as yet to decide between the two alternatives, which indeed are not mutually exclusive. On the whole, the evidence seems to favour a central European origin for some types of timberwork.

Although for convenience some attempt is made to discuss rampart design in a structurally logical way, the result does not correspond, so far as is known, to the chronological sequence in this country, and moreover imposes on the material a fictitious appearance of orderly development. The builders would have available a repertoire of methods, some of which would at any period be more fashionable than others, and radical innovations would be unlikely. Their primary objective must almost always have been to provide an effective defence as economically as possible. Occasionally a desire for display may have played some part in the design.

The simplest defence of all, when timber is available, is a strong fence or palisade. This has been found at many places, especially near the Scottish border; it is not yet certain whether its apparent frequency in that region is real, or due to the accident of discovery and preservation. The posts are usually found to have been spaced, presumably merely to economize on timber. Such an arrangement is likely to have been primarily to keep out animals or casual thieves, for it gives the defenders no advantage in height against any determined attackers.

Sometimes there are two lines of palisade, roughly parallel, 10 metres or more apart, so that the plan is comparable with a small multivallate hill-fort in the same region, such as Dunsinane. Often each circuit of palisading is double, comprising two parallel lines 2 or 3 metres apart. This arrangement could in theory have supported a fighting platform, but more probably its function was to prevent a marauding animal getting the run needed to jump the fence. Enclosures protected only by palisades can therefore hardly be classed as fortified, though many were later given more permanent defences. Effective ramparts could be built entirely of timbers laid horizontally, and have been demonstrated abroad on some waterlogged sites. They would leave no surface traces on dry ground, and have not yet been identified in Britain.

In rocky country, when protection is needed, the idea of a plain wall with built faces using stone gathered on the surface seems obvious. To give the defenders access to the top, the most convenient method is to build the back in steps, sometimes supplemented by ramps as at Tre'r Ceiri (fig. 4). This profile has the added advantage that less stone is used for a given height without reducing the thickness at the base where the wall is vulnerable to attack. The steps are almost always at least 0·5 metres in height, usually more. Ordinary stairs are recorded only in the Scottish duns, and stairs of stones projecting from a nearly vertical wall face seem to be post-Roman, as in the small fort at Garn Boduan.

The third obvious way of making a rampart is to dig a ditch and pile the excavated material on the inner side, giving the glacis type of construction as found at Maiden Castle in its second phase (pl. 3). The bank there was so high and steep that scaling was almost impossible, and the front of the level summit was unprotected, presumably to avoid hindering the slingers. There was a palisade along the back, which is unusual, but whether this was to prevent them stepping incautiously onto the rearward slope during the heat of battle, or to keep children and animals off the wall walk, must remain conjectural. Some banks of this type carried a breastwork of timber or stone near the summit, but most are too eroded for the traces to survive.

Earth and timber separately are not capable of much further elaboration, but stone can be made a more effective or economical defence in several ways. It must have been realized very soon that when the facing collapsed, either owing to accident or to attack, the resulting slope left an easy way onto the rampart; this trouble was to some extent overcome by building an inner face behind the visible outer face, a system generally regarded as the arrangement mentioned by Caesar as *murus duplex*; but its use goes back far beyond

Fig. 4   Types of rampart: Tre'r Ceiri, Worlebury, Cissbury.

his time. The principle can be extended by building several internal faces. Worlebury (fig. 4) is the most elaborate example. Unfortunately it is uncertain whether the facings there were built sinuously to serve some special function, or merely because, as concealed reinforcement, their exact line did not matter. Usually the inner lines run parallel to the main wall face, and this type of construction is found as far afield as southern France.

Although they are outside the scope of this book the galleried duns and brochs of Scotland must be mentioned here. They carry the elaboration and economy of stone architecture still further, by leaving tunnels in the walls, roofed with large slabs. These may be utilized for rooms, passages or stairways, or may be merely structural.

They do not seem to occur in enclosures large enough to be termed hill-forts.

As noted above, simple banks of upcast from a ditch only become effective barriers if they are very high; otherwise an impetuous charge can carry some attackers to the summit. So a vertical or nearly vertical outer face is an advantage for defence, while a similar inner face makes a higher rampart possible for a given volume of excavation.

The simplest way of forming a vertical face using timber is to heap the earth behind a deeply founded palisade of close-set vertical posts. This was used at Cissbury (fig. 4) and at Staple Howe, where the revetment was set some way down a steep slope, and probably tied by horizontal timbers to a row of posts set further back. More commonly, the vertical posts were widely spaced and accompanied by another row at the back of the rampart; again, although not essential, transverse horizontal timbers may be inferred, and traces have occasionally been found. The type site for this sort of timbering is Preist, at Bitburg in the Rhineland. There the revetment was completed by panels of stone walling between the uprights, but this is uncommon in Britain: it has been found at Maiden Castle and South Cadbury. On other sites, such as Wandlebury (fig. 5) or Grimthorpe,

Fig. 5   Types of rampart: Wandlebury.

a revetment of horizontal timbers must have been supported by the uprights, though this need not have been carried right down to the bottom of the bank. An open framework supporting a fighting platform above the bank is theoretically possible, but would have been very vulnerable to attack by fire. Usually, the posts in both rows were vertical. At South Cadbury, where the rows were unusually close, some in the rear row were inclined forwards, but usually there is no need to postulate diagonal timbers; such an arrangement would in fact be a disadvantage, for the wedge of earth above the inclined member would tend to push its top forwards as the material compacted.

There are great variations in the dimensions of this type of construction, ranging from 2 to nearly 5 metres between posts in one row, and similarly between rows, though for any given fort the setting out usually remains fairly uniform. Dr I. M. Stead, in discussing Grimthorpe, has suggested that the narrower ramparts correspond to fortifications thrown up hastily in an emergency. This is certainly the impression given by the structure at Ivinghoe Beacon, where the spacing of posts in each row varies from 2 to 4·5 metres and the rows are not parallel, usually 2 metres apart but sometimes converging to a metre. The fort appears to belong to the Late Bronze Age. Stanford includes it in his scheme for the Marches (p. 73) at S 740, and suggests that the Ffridd Faldwyn 'box rampart' − the general term for this arrangement − should be assigned to S 800.

Where stone was available, either on the surface or from the ditch excavations, a single or double facing of dry masonry without timber uprights could be used as a revetment, whether the filling was of earth or rubble. It must rapidly have become obvious that unless exceptionally well built the repeated effects of frost, or even a heavy rainstorm, could push the upper courses of the revetment outwards and overturn it. The need to tie the facing into the body of the rampart is thus even greater for this type of construction than for a timber revetment, and examples of beams running across the line of wall are quite common. There are two main variants in Britain, in which the ends of the transverse timbers are concealed behind the facing as at Maiden Castle, Bickerton, or exposed as at Castle Law, Abernethy (fig. 6). The latter arrangement seems to have been preferred throughout Scotland. It was remarkably vulnerable to fire, for out of nearly 260 known hill-forts north of the Forth-Clyde isthmus forty-eight show traces of having been burned, which casts

Rainsborough

Castle Law

METRES

Fig. 6   Types   of   rampart: Castle   Law   (Abernethy),
         Rainsborough.

some doubt on the accepted view that the climate during the Iron Age was no drier than it is today. The burning was often so intense that the material of the rampart is vitrified. This was formerly regarded as an intentional attempt to consolidate the wall, but is now accepted as evidence of destruction, either accidental or deliberate.

There are many variations on these basic designs. At Dinorben, the earliest rampart was reinforced not by separate beams but by continuous layers of timber. This is of particular interest, for radiocarbon dating shows that it belongs to about the seventh century BC, and a similar arrangement was found at the Wittnauer Horn in Switzerland. By contrast, Burghead, long believed to be the nearest British parallel to true *murus gallicus* (see below), has now been shown by radiocarbon dating to belong to the sixth or eighth century AD.

Most hill-fort builders adopted some well tried and widely used type of rampart, but occasional exceptions are found. Rainsborough, for example (fig. 6), seems, so far as is known at present, to be unique. The rampart was built in three stages. The lowest was 7·3 metres wide and 0·8 metre high revetted with dry-built facing, the interior filled with crumbled soft limestone; the top was flat, laced with a layer of branches laid transversely and levelled up with turf. On this level surface was built a closely similar second stage, though only 5·5 metres wide, and (probably) filled with turf; it was set almost symmetrically, so that there were steps 0·9 metre and 0·8 metre wide at back and front, respectively. The third stage was again similar, but only about 3·5 metres wide, with filling to a depth of 0·2 metre, so that the revetments, which were about 0·5 metre high, formed low parapets on each side of the rampart walk. There seems no need to follow the excavator in postulating a wooden breastwork, for the structure is early (H 450) and missile weapons would at that period be of little importance. The rear steps were not left level, but were covered by fairly steeply sloping banks of turf or hard sand, and it may be inferred that the front (now mostly destroyed) was similar, so that the face towards the enemy would form an alternation of steep slopes and low vertical walls. This remarkable rampart was part of a bivallate system of defences, a surprisingly complex arrangement for such an early date, and apparently unconnected with the use of the sling.

Before leaving the details of rampart construction, the accepted form of classic *murus gallicus* – the 'Avaricum' type – must be described, though it is apparently unknown in Britain. Substantial beams are laid, evenly spaced, on the ground or on a prepared platform with their lengths transversely to the line of the wall, and the intervals levelled up with earth or rubble. The next layer is formed of beams similarly spaced, but set longitudinally; each is pinned to the lower beam with a long iron spike, and the intervals are again filled. This procedure is repeated, using transverse and longitudinal beams alternately, until the required height is reached. The beam ends are usually exposed in the front revetment. Caesar describes this construction in detail, and says that it is resistant both to the battering ram and to fire; but some walls of this type are found vitrified in France. The essential diagnostic feature is the presence of the long iron spikes used to pin the beams together.

In multivallate forts, the subsidiary ramparts use the same structural methods as the main banks but are generally less elaborate. Wandlebury (fig. 5) is an interesting example where the outer bank of the bivallate fort was superimposed on the ruins of an earlier single rampart. Both were timber revetted, but the details differed.

The presence of a berm between bank and ditch is almost essential where the rampart face is revetted, to prevent collapse. Whether there is any cultural significance in its width remains uncertain.

Ditches vary in form, but again there is nothing to indicate a cultural distinction between those which are V-shaped and those with flat bottoms. The difference probably depends in most cases merely on the nature of the material to be excavated. The use of a single rampart with an exceptionally broad flat-bottomed ditch (the Fécamp type, p. 48) does seem to be a distinctive and late feature.

At almost all hill-forts, banks, walls and ditches provide all the elements used in defence, but rarely these are supplemented by *chevaux-de-frise* of small pointed stones set upright. This has been discussed above (pp. 48–9).

There is one other form of supplementary defence which should be mentioned here. Mr Forde-Johnston has drawn attention to several cases where a large hill-fort is accompanied by a smaller one some distance away which commands ground concealed from observation by the occupants of the larger site. He has suggested that these are deliberate tactical arrangements, to provide advance warning of attack. From a modern point of view, it would seem that a couple of sentries would serve the same purpose, without diminishing the numbers available to defend the main enclosure. Moreover, whereas a small party in the open might reasonably hope to gain safety after the enemy were sighted, those in a relatively weak advanced fort would be almost suicidally trapped. These arguments do not necessarily discredit the theory, for the tactical principles adopted in the Iron Age were not those of today; but it is difficult to see how the hypothesis could be tested.

The most vulnerable parts of a hill-fort's defences were the gateways, for once the timber gate was destroyed by fire or battered down the way into the enclosure lay open. They are also the places where any desire for display can be most fully manifested. Hill-fort entrances thus tend to be elaborate and interesting. Further, since a gateway where the timber has rotted is worse than useless, they are more likely to retain evidence of repair and reconstruction than other parts of the defences; so particularly important information can be recovered by skilled excavation (as at Croft Ambrey), or destroyed if the work is done badly.

Functionally, the entrance arrangements fall into three parts. There is the gate itself, with the framing for its support; associated works within the enclosure, such as guard chambers; and the approaches outside the gateway.

Nothing recognizable has survived to show the actual form of any gate. They were of timber, usually entirely so; occasionally some fragments of possible iron fitments survive, but even nails are rare. The simplest were probably merely movable shutters, for some gateways show no trace of any framing to which a gate could have been hinged. Such a shutter would have been unmanageably heavy for any opening more than about 1·5 metres wide, but would have been perfectly adequate for the narrow entrances of some stone forts. Some gateways may have been closed only in emergencies. At Croft Ambrey a slot across the gateway can best be interpreted as intended to take the ends of upright posts; at this sophisticated fortress, these would have supplemented a hinged gate. Caesar notes that the entrances to Bigberry were blocked by tree trunks set close together. In stone forts gateways are often found walled up, as at Duchary Rock or Garn Boduan, and it may well be that smaller openings were normally closed in this way, but only when necessary.

Where evidence is found for a wooden frame some sort of gate can be be inferred, especially where guard houses exist, and for wide openings

Dinorben

Phase I & II

METRES

Phase III & IV

Fig. 7 Gateways: Dinorben, earlier phases.

some sort of hinged support may be postulated. The details must remain guesswork, for all timber has vanished. The iron ring for a
pivot was found at Hembury, but these are extremely uncommon, as
are holed stones which might have been sockets. In the absence of
evidence it is fruitless to speculate as to the exact arrangement, but
the builders must have been capable of devising some fairly efficient

Dinorben
Phase V

METRES

*Fig. 8 Gateways: Dinorben,
latest phase.*

hanging for gates. Leaves up to 2·5 metres wide and high can be inferred, and unless hinged so that the moving edge was off the ground these would have needed two or three men to drag them open.

For any large hinged gate, a lintel to complete the frame would be almost essential. This leads naturally to the idea of a bridge to carry the rampart walk across the entrance gap. The usual arrangement seems likely to have been that suggested in Rainsborough, with the front of the bridge immediately over the gate. Sometimes, nevertheless, the bridge was set well in front of the gate. Bredon Hill provides the clearest example of this. At that gateway, too, there was good reason to believe that the lintel − not, in this case, the bridge − was ornamented with a row of severed heads (fig. 9).

Some sort of controlling authority is implied by the decision to build a rampart, even if no more than an *ad hoc* 'council of elders'. So some formal delegation of responsibility for the control of the gate is to be expected, to the forerunners of the 'proud porters' of medieval and later ballads and romances. Archaeologically, this leaves its trace in the presence of some building which can be interpreted as a guard house.

This need be no more than a small recess, such as the 'sentry boxes' at the east entrance of Maiden Castle in its last pre-Roman phase (pl. 4). These were semicircular in plan, of about 1·5 metres radius, and thus far too small for permanent dwellings, though one had a hearth. They must imply some sort of rota system for gate-keeping. More commonly, the guard houses are as commodious as an ordinary dwelling. Sometimes they are indistinguishable, as at Conway Mountain, where a single round hut was built on to the rampart with its doorway immediately towards the back of the gate passage; the interpretation of this as a guard chamber is merely an inference, though a reasonable one. There can be no doubt about the function of the compartments which are incorporated in the actual planning of the gate passage, as at Rainsborough or Dinorben (figs 7 and 10). In such gateways, the guard houses are almost always paired, and often show as much evidence of occupation as the houses within the fort. It seems a legitimate conjecture that sometimes, at least, they were in fact family dwellings, the tenure carrying with it responsibilities for control of the gate; and that the pairing was to ensure that the entrance need never be left unattended.

At Rainsborough, there was a large freestanding post on each side of the entrance passage, just behind the back of the ramparts; in view

Bredon Hill Gateway

Fig. 9 Gateways: Bredon Hill.

of this evidence, two pits at St Catherine's Hill can be interpreted in the same way. No practical function can be suggested for these. They may have carried a lintel, forming a 'triumphal arch', as suggested by M. Avery for Rainsborough, though no skulls were found in association; or they may have been carved or decorated, by analogy with Indian totem poles. The carving on the lintel sketched in the reconstruction (fig. 10) is wholly conjectural.

The greatest elaboration of entrance arrangements took place outside the actual gate. From the practical standpoint, the objectives were twofold: to prevent a direct rush at the gate; and to force any-one approaching to follow a route commanded by the occupants of the fort. Sometimes, in addition, the plan seems to have been influenced by a desire for display. At Maiden Castle, for example, the complexity of the entrances in their last phase can hardly be accounted for purely by the needs of defence. On the other hand, forts with quite elaborate and sophisticated ramparts and gateways may be content with a simple straight approach to the actual gate, as at Rainsborough.

The simplest way of satisfying the two primary requirements, given a second line of defence, is to place the entrance through the outer rampart to one side of that through the inner. Chun Castle shows a typical example of this scheme applied to a small stone fort. Forcing the line of approach to turn through an angle almost inevitably results in a passage commanded from the ramparts, though only from one side.

If a straight approach was accepted as satisfactory, the gate might be placed at the inner end of a long passage. In its simplest form, this passage is formed by inturning the main ramparts, as at The Wrekin; the whole plan is merely a development of the ordinary gate passage with guard chambers. A more elaborate arrangement, often an addition to an earlier fort, is the barbican, in which a roughly triangular extension is built outwards on each side of the entrance, leaving a long narrow passage to approach the gate. The most perfect example of this type is that at Blackbury Castle; Maiden Castle, phase two, had a similar scheme, but with a double gate.

The ramparts at the entrance were sometimes given a projection to form a bastion commanding the gateway. At Blackbury they seem to have preceded the barbican, and to have been well shaped and paired as at a medieval castle gateway; but nearly all the known examples in Britain seem to have been single, and to have formed an ill defined bulge rather than a precise D-shaped projection. The best are perhaps

Fig. 10   Gateways: St Catherine's Hill, Rainsborough.

at Dinorben and Mynydd Bychan, but many may exist unrecognized, their rather vague original outline having become obscured by erosion. The slingers' platforms in the east entrance of Maiden Castle, phase four, probably served a similar purpose, to give command over the approaches. The extreme rarity of any parallels must be due to the accidents of discovery.

The hill-fort builders were no more doctrinaire in the details of entrance design than in other parts of their work. In general, they were content to do as little as seemed necessary to provide a defensible entrance, using natural features where appropriate, as in the curving approach up the hillside to Chalbury, overlooked from above, or by running the entrance approach along the edge of a steep hillside. Nevertheless, they sometimes undertook work of great elaboration, such as the exceptionally long inturns at Bredon Hill (fig. 29), or the complex approaches to Maiden Castle. Sites such as the last provide some of the most spectacular earthworks in Britain, but they are not typical. Neither are all outworks defensive. Lightly built walls or fences may have been needed to direct cattle towards the entrance, to keep them off adjacent fields, or to form pens. Usually such minor works have been destroyed, but good examples survive at Lordenshaws in Northumberland.

Potentially, the changes in gateway design can provide one of the most important elements in a broad chronological and cultural framework. Dr Stanford has suggested the following development in the Welsh Marches (see p. 99). Initially (S 750) the box rampart fort at Ffridd Faldwyn had a single portal. About a century later, twin portals came into fashion, to be superseded once again by single portals during the period S 350 to S 300. The twin guard rooms which are such a striking feature of hill-forts in this region came into use in S 400, and remained in fashion until S 270, initially in timber and for the last half-century in stone. The decline of the guard room system is thus roughly contemporary with the reversion from double to single portals. Finally, in S 60, the practice of bridging the gate passage came into use. This scheme, as Dr Stanford emphasizes, is a tentative one, but it is based on careful and detailed excavations at several forts; it does not introduce any very serious difficulties when extended outside the Marches. Perhaps the very late date assigned to the introduction of a bridge may be doubted; it seems such an obvious and natural modification, and the question whether posts did or did not support a gangway cannot easily be resolved.

10

The Interior

Except in temporary refuges or cattle kraals, where tents might have served, any hill-fort must have contained more or less permanent dwellings, as well as associated structures. The characteristic building in British hill-forts was round, usually of 6 to 8 metres diameter internally, though some Iron Age houses are as much as 15 metres across; the best known example of these large dwellings is that at Little Woodbury, probably built before any rampart was contemplated there. The smaller dwellings are usually referred to in a rather derogatory way as 'huts'; indeed, the term 'hut circle' is so well established that to retain it is probably better than to attempt to replace it. All the same, it gives a very misleading impression, as can be seen by comparison with modern houses. Omitting passage and bathroom, but including the kitchen, a two-bedroom bungalow of a type selling at between £8,000 and £10,000 in 1974 has a total area equivalent to a round 'hut' of just over 7 metres diameter, while even for a larger house, with three bedrooms and two reception rooms and selling at between £20,000 and £25,000, the diameter would be less than 10 metres.

An adequate account of Iron Age round houses would require, and deserve, a book to itself. The commonest internal arrangement, to which there are many exceptions, consisted of a ring of posts set upright about 1·5 to 2 metres inside the line of the wall. These served to support the roof timbers and formed a natural division between the central living space, with a hearth near the middle, and sleeping compartments against the wall. By analogy with dwellings in the north built exclusively of stone, these compartments were probably separated by hangings or boarded partitions which have left no trace. To visualize the sort of accommodation which could be provided by quite a small 'hut', 7 metres in diameter, one may assume a central living space 4 metres across. This leaves room for an entrance passage 1·3 metres wide and five sleeping compartments each 1·5 metres wide and tapering from over 4 metres long at the house wall to 2·6 metres at the inner side. It must be repeated that this is merely illustrative. There was great variety in structure and in internal arrangement. Since the object here is to indicate the general character of the settlement, no attempt has been made to illustrate these in detail.

Outside, all these round houses must have looked very much alike. Their walls were of wood, dry-stone or cob according to locality, and probably stood at most only 1·5 metres high, usually less than a metre to judge from stone examples. Above this rose a conical roof, perhaps truncated over very large houses to allow for a central court. The material was probably of thatch in most cases, but sometimes of turf. Occasionally there is evidence, from a drip mark, of wide eaves, but some relatively modern Scottish dwellings show that the occupants of simple buildings are not always concerned to avoid mere dampness, so in some, especially those of stone, the roof covering may have ended about the middle of the wall. Often a ditch was dug round the house to intercept surface water; this may have coincided with the drip from the thatch, but need not have done so. The only break in this plain conical outline would be at the entrance, sometimes no more than a simple gap, or a doorway between two uprights, but occasionally quite an elaborate projecting porch.

We have no direct knowledge of the finish of these houses, and reconstructions, whether drawn or three-dimensional, almost always show them as built of rough timbers, and shaggy with untrimmed thatch. No doubt some were of this character, but although the builders lacked lime mortar, their dry-stone masonry and their carpentry were of a standard just as high as that of the Middle Ages; and they had a sophisticated decorative art. It is reasonable to suppose, therefore, that many of their houses would display as high a technical finish as the dwelling of a prosperous farmer in later times, or a small medieval manor house. It is tempting to suggest that the woodwork was sometimes embellished with carving, but no evidence for ornamental work on building timbers of this date has ever been recorded in Britain.

During the later 1930s, the excavation of Little Woodbury first displayed convincingly all the structural remains which could be left by an Iron Age farm. With the recognition there that granaries were' implied by four post holes set in a square (see below), the roundness of the houses of the British Iron Age became for many archaeologists a matter of dogma. Rectangular houses identified at Maiden Castle were explained away as misinterpretations of the evidence, and the parallel rows of post holes uncovered at Ffridd Faldwyn were regarded as inexplicable by the excavator and ignored by others; interpreted as granaries they would have implied an incredible concentration of corn-growing in that region. Recently, however, Dr Stanford's work at Croft Ambrey and elsewhere has demonstrated that square or rectangular dwellings are the only type found in some forts in the Welsh Marches, while in other parts of Britain they occur mixed, but not necessarily contemporary, with round houses. The Ffridd Faldwyn posts can now be understood as evidence for rows of small square buildings, which have been found also at Croft Ambrey. Elsewhere the rectangular buildings are sometimes larger. One rather irregular one at Maiden Castle measured 4·5 by 6 metres, and was divided into two rooms; one longer side was adjacent to a contemporary street. Other rectangular buildings could be identified there, but later structures had disturbed the area too much for the whole arrangement to be worked out.

The problem of the relationship between round and rectangular houses has not yet been solved. There is some indication that where both occur together on the same site the rectangles are the earlier. This is curious, as the round ones are generally regarded as in the Bronze Age tradition, and the others as intrusive. Pending further research, a tentative explanation could be that the rectangular houses correspond to an actual massive settlement of invaders, not merely the intrusion of foreign ideas, and that where round houses occur later there has been a renaissance of the influence of the earlier traditions, just as the official use of English reappeared after an interlude of Norman French.

Most of these dwellings survive, if at all, as levelled platforms terraced into hill slopes. Sometimes the rectangular buildings stood on recognizably elongated terraces, but at other sites the builders inconsiderately erected them on rounded platforms, so unless actual walls exist (and not always then) the predominant type of house cannot be determined from surface evidence; though it may be fairly safe to assume round houses if *all* the platforms are circular. Thus most of the evidence for the intensity of occupation and the disposition of buildings comes from regions where stone was normally used for building, and cannot be taken to apply exactly elsewhere. Fortunately, a few places such as Hod Hill, Hambledon Hill or Chalbury in southern Britain preserve the evidence in visible form, and at several on either side of the Scottish border the slots in which the timber walls stood can still be traced in the fine turf.

For round houses, the clearest evidence comes from some Caernarvonshire forts, such as Garn Boduan or Conway Mountain; both, unfortunately, are of two periods. Tre'r Ceiri (pl. 5), in the first phase, was a smaller hill-fort of the same type. The buildings are all round, and seem to have been placed in any convenient position without regard to possible trackways; the roughly aligned rows are related to the shape of the ground. This seems to apply equally to Hambledon Hill. At Hod Hill, in the surviving part, the arrangement looks random, but the aerial photograph taken before 1939 shows that there were two well defined streets curving from the north-east gateway through the mass of houses. Similarly at Maiden Castle, though the plan could not be traced, a street led from the east gate to a round building which may have been a temple (see below). Streets, where they existed, seem to have been marked out at a fairly early stage in the life of the fort, but there was no formal town-planning associated with the round houses.

In Garn Boduan and Conway Mountain there were from eight to twelve dwellings per hectare, depending on the assumptions made as to how many houses belonged to each period. This seems to be fairly typical of southern Britain, where evidence survives; the undamaged part of Hod Hill, for example, has some fifteen buildings per hectare. In Scotland, the density seems generally to be about twice this. Even in the south, though, the rule is not universal. At Moel Trigarn there are well over forty house platforms per hectare, but that is unusual.

At forts with square houses regularly arranged, such as Croft Ambrey (pl. 7) and Ffridd Faldwyn, conditions are very different. There, where the form of the ground permits, the little buildings are laid out deliberately in streets and are far more closely set, so that there may be as many as fifty or sixty per hectare. Their regularity of arrangement, and uniformity in character, have led Dr Stanford to suggest for consideration the possibility that they may correspond to barracks, forts where they occur being the centres where young warriors received their initiation and training. It is noteworthy that extensive testing of the enclosure at Croft Ambrey failed to discover any place where the small standardized dwellings gave way to some more spacious building which could be claimed as the 'chief's house'.

Conclusions as to the arrangement of the buildings and other structures in a hill-fort almost always depend on inferences, either from those features which were substantial enough to remain visible or from partial excavation. Total clearance is very uncommon. Walesland Rath therefore needs to be mentioned here, though primarily as an example of the extreme complexity which may be displayed by a superficially simple enclosure. Unfortunately, despite the exemplary care with which the excavation was conducted, it is impossible convincingly to separate out the different features so as to reconstruct the nature of the settlement in any particular phase.

Although 'hut circles', interpreted as the emplacements of houses, are generally the only features which remain visible, excavation of an intensively occupied fort, at least in the south, will usually reveal a confused medley of pits, gullies and post holes. Little Woodbury and Walesland Rath are examples which have been extensively cleared. Regular pits are now accepted as having been intended mostly for the storage of grain for consumption. When they became too sour for this they were used as rubbish dumps. Seed corn was stored in granaries above ground, now represented by four post holes set at the corners of a square, and thus not readily differentiated from a square house. For an isolated structure, the distinction can often be no more than guesswork, unless grain is actually present. Pairs of posts can be interpreted as drying racks, either for fodder or for corn which has had to be reaped unripe. Both these types of structure still survive in parts of Europe. Even when all allowance has been made for 'granaries' and 'drying racks', many post holes usually remain unaccounted for. Too little is known about the development of most forts, but the evidence from Maiden Castle suggests that in earlier periods disused storage pits half filled with decaying rubbish must have been an appreciable hazard to persons moving between the dwellings. Presumably, though, even at night, the smell would serve as a warning.

Temples dating from the Roman period are found in some hill-forts, and it is a reasonable inference that they are often the direct successors of earlier sacred sites; but these can seldom be identified with certainty. Maiden Castle offers an example which illustrates very well the problems of such an identification.

The main street from the east gate led directly to the doorway of a round 'hut', rather large but otherwise perfectly normal; but excavation indicated that the 'hut' was of the latest pre-Roman phase, Iron Age C, and that the road was not then in use. Apart from any question of religious function, there is thus an immediate problem: why was the track laid out to lead to the entrance to a building which had not then been built? Or, conversely, why was the hut located symmetrically relative to a disused road? Within the ruined outline of this 'hut' was a roughly built round structure of similar character, rather smaller, dated by numerous (171) coins to about AD 350–60. Among the debris on the floor was the base of a statuette, and in the edge of one of the holes for roof supports was another. Beneath the floor was a sparse scatter of objects which filled rather thinly the chronological interval between the Belgic and Roman 'huts'. There is nothing incontrovertibly religious about these buildings, but 12 metres north-east of them is an indisputable temple, built some ten or twenty years later than the Roman 'round hut'. Professor Piggott has pointed out that just west of this Romano-Celtic temple is a setting of four posts which can be paralleled exactly on sites abroad which are undoubtedly religious; unfortunately they can be paralleled equally exactly by posthole settings in this country which are universally accepted as the remains of granaries.

This is the evidence in summary. The writer feels no doubt whatever, as a matter of personal belief, that the whole area was a sacred centre from the establishment of the hill-fort; that there was direct continuity of sanctity right through to the end of the Roman period; and that the Roman round building was displayed to the pious but gullible visitor as the original shrine. The only difficulty in this interpretation is to understand how the attendant guides could have allowed 171 coins to slip through their fingers. Whatever one may believe as an individual, though, none of this can be maintained as having been scientifically demonstrated; the apparent 'evidence' need be no more than an assembly of coincidences. The rational approach must be that adopted by Sir Mortimer Wheeler in his excavation report, where, after setting out the facts given above, he says that all this 'justifies perhaps the passing fantasy' that there was continuity of cult at this spot.

Rarely, there are fully convincing indications of a pre-Roman Sanctuary, as at South Cadbury, where a rectangular building of unusual plan was approached between two rows of large pits each of which contained, at the bottom, an animal skull. The conclusive identification of this temple was the result not merely of careful and extensive excavation, but of the flair which enabled the excavator to choose the right place to dig. The lack of recorded pre-Roman shrines is thus no guide as to whether they were normal or exceptional. It is a reasonable hypothesis that even in the smallest settlements some supernatural protection would be considered desirable, and where the population was large enough a permanent temple might be expected. The names of some forts may indicate the deities worshipped (pp. 17–19), though we can know nothing of the ritual; and the occasional evidence for temples of Roman date seems to imply continued sanctity, even after the general population had moved away. On the other hand, solid proof is hardly obtainable. The early shrines were not necessarily structurally different in any way from ordinary dwellings, so that even where almost all the building foundations survive, as at Garn Boduan, there is no way in which one can be picked out as a probable temple. Even excavation may not provide conclusive evidence, for the associated ritual need not have been of a kind which left recognizable traces.

Celtic sanctuaries were not always marked by buildings. The worship of springs is well attested, but is not likely to be represented within a hill-top settlement. Another type of religious structure, perhaps the oddest from a modern viewpoint, was a deep shaft, down which sacrifices could be despatched to the underworld. Examples (earlier than the ramparts) have recently been discovered at Danebury, and no doubt others have been overlooked or dismissed as wells. Again, only extensive excavations can determine how often these sacred shafts occur. The extent to which hill-forts were religious centres must for the present remain a matter for guesswork.

So far as major secular buildings are concerned, there is seldom material even for guesses. One may suppose that the greater fortresses provided for a chieftain, but superficially there is little to choose between one dwelling and another. The suggestion that a pair of buildings excavated at Hod Hill belonged to the chief is attractive, and is supported by the fact that they were the targets of attack by ballista, and that one stands in a separate compound at the end of one of the main streets of the settlement. On consideration, though, the argument does not stand. The presence of a separate compound is relatively unusual on that site, but there were other and larger examples; other buildings also are considerably larger; and since only five or six dwellings were investigated out of an original total of some five hundred or more it is impossible to maintain that the presence of the ballista bolts necessarily imples that these huts were of particular importance.

This egalitarian character of Iron Age housing seems fairly general, but as with other aspects of the subject it is unsafe to generalize. At South Cadbury some of the houses found near the temple were exceptionally large, some 10·5 metres in diameter and thus of about twice the floor area of the usual 'hut'. So it may be merely a matter of luck that the dwellings of the aristocracy have escaped recognition, at least in the regions where timber buildings were normal.

Irish traditions would imply not only a chief's dwelling but a possible separate banqueting hall. The large central round building at Clickhimin has been claimed as an example of this, and it is indeed a striking and distinctive structure, from which the associated dwellings are recognizably very different. No really satisfactory parallel has yet been claimed at any fort on the British mainland, so the southward extension of this sort of social organization must remain a matter for conjecture. It is tempting to recognize something similar in Walesland Rath, but despite, or perhaps because of, the care and completeness with which that site was excavated, its interpretation presents great difficulty.

11

The Romans and After

With the arrival of the Romans, archaeology in Britain seems to emerge from the mists of estimated dates and vague regional cultures into a clear landscape in which everything is sharp and well defined. The clarity of the view wavers a little under close inspection, but to a great extent it is genuine; there is a background of historical information, and the mass production of coins and pottery makes it possible to establish fairly reliable chronological links throughout the empire.

Hill-forts remain on the fringe of this well-systematized archaeology. In fully Romanized areas they were disused; new ones were built or old ones re-occupied only where central authority did not reach or where it broke down. Their development can sometimes be worked out in relation to the history of Roman Britain, but seldom with the same precision. Moreover, the Roman occupation was incomplete, and differed in character and duration in different regions; and its start and finish were long drawn out. To understand its influence on hill-fort building a summary is necessary, though this is unavoidably very much over-simplified.

For the Victorians, these islands entered history with the invasions of Julius Caesar. His attack, almost certainly on Bigberry in Kent, is the first record of a British hill-fort. Otherwise, archaeologically, his activities have left no structural trace as yet discovered. Full-scale invasion began nearly a century later, in AD 43. It was by no means a walkover, even though some regions, such as Sussex, willingly accepted the status of allies; but the most prosperous part of the country, south-east of the line from Severn to Trent, was under fairly secure control by AD 50. The historical record, that the general Vespasian overcame twenty towns, is vividly illuminated by the war cemetery at Maiden Castle, and the Roman fort built within the native fortress at Hod Hill. The destruction of the gateway at South Cadbury was witness to some later, unrecorded incident. These contrast strongly with the lack of anything of that kind in the downland forts of Sussex. Even in hostile regions the old hill-forts were not always forcibly cleared, but the attractions of the new Roman towns led to their evacuation within a decade or so, save perhaps for priests still tending an ancient shrine.

Further advances, mostly into wild or mountainous country, were more strongly resisted, and the whole region south of the Tyne-Solway isthmus was not brought fully under control for another thirty years, so some hill-forts north and west of the Severn-Trent line may well have remained in use for a generation after the initial invasion. After the Tyne-Solway isthmus was reached, the land to the south remained part of the empire until the end of the fourth century AD, and no hill-forts are likely to have been built or refortified there during that time, though some may have remained inhabited.

Further north, conditions were more complex. Initially, the advance continued, reaching the edge of the highlands by AD 84, when the Caledonians were defeated at the unlocated battle of Mons Graupius, but after about fifteen years the frontier was withdrawn to the Tyne-Solway line, where in about AD 120 the emperor Hadrian ordered the construction of the wall which is known by his name. After another two decades the frontier was advanced again, and a wall of turf – the Antonine Wall – built across the Clyde-Forth isthmus. Finally, in about AD 180, the troops withdrew once more to Hadrian's line, probably after treaty arrangements with the tribes between the walls. In that region, then, there were two intervals when hill-forts might be built or used; in the first by enemies to the Romans, in the second and longer period by allies.

North of the Forth–Clyde line, despite several decisive Roman victories recorded in Roman sources, the natives were never brought under the control of the invaders. No doubt evidence of slighting remains to be discovered in some hill-forts, and objects of Roman date, from trade or looting, have been found in several, showing their continued use. New types, discussed below, developed both here and further south.

The more noteworthy traces of the Roman conquest of southern Britain have already been mentioned, as at Maiden Castle and South Cadbury. Hod Hill is of especial interest, for the ramparts of the Roman fortress can still be seen superimposed on the earlier hill-fort. This conjunction is unique in Britain, and very rare anywhere. Moving further west, into the areas conquered later, evidence for massacres has been found at Bredon Hill and at Sutton Walls, but these were not certainly the work of Roman troops. Massacre of the defeated was not normal Roman practice, either because of genuine humanity or because it was wasteful to destroy financially valuable slaves; but if the heads over the gateway at Bredon Hill were those of captured Romans, the nature of the other remains found there would be explicable. The evidence which the hill-forts offer is usually less dramatic. Hod Hill, for example, displays outworks which were begun too late and never completed; but works of this kind cannot easily be identified from surface evidence.

In the north and west, where the Roman presence was primarily military, some hill-forts show indications of use for field training exercises. At Caer y Twr, above Holyhead in Anglesey, a short length of wall has been cast down; it is deliberate slighting, but could have been rebuilt in a day, and the length is far too small to have much effect on the strength of the defences. Burnswark, in Dumfriesshire, was for long believed to have been the subject of a full-scale siege. Sling bullets of baked clay have been found within the ramparts, and at the foot of the hill the regular forts of the attackers are still visible. Nineteenth-century archaeologists believed they could also trace a circumvallation, but this is now generally accepted as a misinterpretation of recent field banks.

This important site has now been re-examined by Mr Jobey, who has shown that this dramatic story was true, save for one point: the whole attack was directed against a hill-fort which had been abandoned for many years.

Still in the borders, but further east, another example of practice siege-works can be seen at Woden Law. There, genuine lines of circumvallation, apparently from two different campaigns of field exercises, would have cut off the inhabitants from any chance of escape — but again the native fort was almost certainly empty at the time.

The Britons do not seem to have practised siege warfare, so we cannot expect to find traces of their work impinging in a comparable way on Roman forts; but there is one case known, at Ruberslaw in Roxburghshire, where a Roman fortlet of some kind was demolished and replaced by a native work. The destruction was so complete that not even the plan of the fortlet can be seen, but characteristic worked stones are used in the native wall. This later work is a 'nuclear fort' (see p. 45), a type which seems to be post-Roman; so the Roman fortlet may well have been in complete ruin when the existing defences were built.

After the conquest, hill-forts in the fully Romanized zone were soon abandoned, the inhabitants moving into newly built towns. Further north and west, in areas under full control but less completely transformed socially, occupation of some forts continued, but so few have been examined that it usually remains unknown whether they remained towns or villages of their old character, or whether merely a few farms continued to exist on the otherwise abandoned site. Two examples which did survive as towns of a sort are described later: Tre'r Ceiri and Traprain Law (pp. 92–9).

The temple in Maiden Castle has been mentioned earlier (p. 79) and other examples are known; they are not in fact very numerous but more probably await discovery. One like the square temple at Maiden Castle has been recorded in Chanctonbury Ring; at Croft Ambrey there is a curious mound, best explicable as the site of a temple that was largely of wood; and a large round timber building of Roman date at Dinorben produced relics which strongly suggest that it was in fact a shrine.

The most remarkable religious establishment in any British hill-fort is that at Lydney in Gloucestershire. The site chosen was within fairly considerable ramparts, where some descendants of the original inhabitants seem to have continued to eke out a living by farming and metalworking. Some time after AD 360 an impressive temple was built, probably the finest in Britain outside a town, accompanied by a guest house and a suite of baths. The temple was a place of healing, and by good fortune inscriptions preserve the name of the deity to whom it was dedicated, Nodens. The shrine seems to have continued prosperous well into the fifth century. It is tantalizing that we can never know what spectacular cure or vision established its fame.

The end of the Roman occupation is more obscure than its beginning, and equally long drawn out. The scraps of semi-historical records cannot all be reconciled into a coherent story, and by judicious selection some can be found to support almost any desired thesis, so until much more archaeological evidence is available detailed discussion of this period is unprofitable. Basically, though, it would appear that under threat from pirates, and from looters out of the unconquered north, the authorities of Britain at the end of the fourth and beginning of the fifth centuries called in mercenaries for their defence – some from abroad, some from between the two

Roman walls, and possibly some from Ireland. Central authority collapsed, and such government as there was fell into the hands of the leaders of local war bands. In some places these were the officers of the foreign mercenaries, in others probably the descendants of legitimate local administrators. The confused traditions of battles and intrigues suggest that the former attempted to extend their rule, and the latter either to maintain their territory or to restore central government. The most successful of these last was 'King Arthur', who gained a unique position in folk memory, so that given a sufficiently uncritical approach evidence of a sort can be found for his presence in almost any part of Britain.

By the time records once more become tolerably reliable, in say the seventh or eighth centuries, the descendants of these local leaders have become royal, each ruling over his own little kingdom; there were six or seven of these in Wales alone. Everyday life must have differed little from that of the pre-Roman period, and such change as there was seems to have been for the worse. Hill-forts once again came into use. In the south-west some at least of the old earthworks were refortified, South Cadbury and probably Castle Dore being among the most notable. These were in a region which had experienced the full benefits of Roman civilization. In Wales some small forts seem to have been built at this time. That on the summit of Garn Boduan is certainly not earlier than the latter part of the Roman period, and could even have been the home of Buan, after whom the hill is named: he lived about the beginning of the seventh century.

Another much larger fort, with its defences dated fairly securely to the mid-fifth century, is Dinas Emrys. This occupies a craggy hill, naturally very strong, but the ramparts are shoddy by Iron Age standards. Its great interest comes from its traditional association with Ambrosius Aurelianus, from whom it takes its name. He was probably a genuine historical character, concerned with the defence of the remnants of Romano-British civilization, and the remarkable and rather improbable piece of fringe history which links his name to the site has been to some extent confirmed by modern excavation (see pp. 186–7). There were no dragons, but there was a pool, and at about the right period a structure had in fact been built beside it! This poses the usual problem in assessing tradition. Did Vortigern really try to build a dwelling on this rather unsuitable foundation? Or did some local storyteller make up the tale to account for what he could see at Dinas Emrys?

In Scotland several fortresses of about this time are mentioned in the chronicles. Dunadd, for example, was captured by the Picts in 736, and Dundurn was besieged in 683. Both are of the curious type known as 'nuclear forts' (see p. 45). As indicated earlier these, so far as is known at present, belong exclusively to this relatively late period. They may be a development from examples, probably earlier, where a small fort has been superimposed on a larger and more ancient enclosure, giving what is functionally the same result as a 'citadel' with base courts.

These seem to be the last structures which can be called hill-forts without straining beyond all reason the use of a term already rather overworked. The idea of a defence using the advantages of a hill top continues even up to the fortresses built round London and Portsmouth in the nineteenth century; but hill-forts can be taken to end, at latest, with the arrival of Norman influences in Britain.

12

Four Important Hill-Forts
Maiden Castle, Tre'r Ceiri, Traprain Law, Croft Ambrey

Faced with the need to select a few hill-forts of particular interest, no two archaeologists would agree; so the writer will not attempt to justify his choice. Nevertheless, there would be wide acceptance of Maiden Castle's claim to take pride of place, though there are at least four major pieces of research in progress which when fully published will threaten its supremacy. It is merely a coincidence, though a happy one, that of the four places chosen one lies in Scotland and one in Wales; the selection was made on other grounds. References to position and to published reports are given in the gazetteer.

Maiden Castle (pl. 2), near Dorchester in Dorset, was the first British hill-fort to be the subject of large-scale *scientific* excavation, and the report remains one of the foundation stones for the archaeology of the Iron Age. As its author recognized, it is not without faults, but these arose from the intervention of a major war, not from defects in method. The war also inhibited the full harvest from the planned ancillary investigations into other forts in southern England and northern France. Despite this, the work has long remained the most important study of its kind. It is only now, after a full generation, that one can look forward to this position being taken, or shared, by other sites.

The natural shape of the hill on which Maiden Castle stands is now disguised by the immense ramparts of the prehistoric town, but was originally a broad ridge with its long axis east and west, the top forming two knolls rising 5 metres or so above an intervening saddle. Occupation of the site began with a neolithic causewayed camp round the eastern knoll. Some time after this had been abandoned, people of the same or of a related culture built an enormous burial mound over the site, 540 metres long and 27 wide, between broad flat-bottomed ditches. All this took place well before 3000 BC. The interval which then elapsed before the arrival of the later fort-

builders was longer than that from the final abandonment of the fort
to the present day.

The new arrivals, about H 300, would have found all the neolithic
structures represented by grassy mounds, the bank of the causewayed camp accentuating a good natural defensive line round the
knoll. Along this line (fig. 11) they dug a great ditch of V profile, 11
metres wide and 6 metres deep, separated by a berm 3 metres wide
from the face of the rampart. This had slightly inclined revetments of
timber to front and rear (cf. fig. 5), a form of construction characteristic of 'Hallstatt' fortifications on the continent. The western
entrance, 5 metres wide, had a pair of gates closing on a central stop,
the passage being revetted in the same way as the rampart; later
disturbance leaves the existence of guard houses uncertain. At the
east end, the entrances were similar, but even at this stage the
designer aimed at a monumental effect, building a pair of gateways
separated by a 20-metre length of rampart. A space nearly 100
metres square outside this double portal was carefully paved with
flint metalling. Traces of timber enclosures here suggest its use as a
market-place.

These early defences were not maintained; the timbers were allowed to decay, and the rampart collapsed into a bank with a steeply
sloping face descending unbroken into the silted ditch. This turf-
covered bank may have suggested the form of rampart used when
about H 200 the inhabitants decided to extend their line of wall to
enclose the whole hilltop (18·5 hectares), for these later ramparts
(and all subsequent reconstructions) were of the glacis type (p. 59).
Excavation at the junction of the earlier enclosure and the extension
not only revealed evidence for their relative age, but was rewarded by
the discovery of a foundation sacrifice, the skeleton of a young man
in his twenties, buried in a pit cut into the front slope of the older
bank and covered (at once, for there was no weathering of the pit
walls) by the material of the extension.

Either as part of the new works, or perhaps rather earlier, the
eastern gateway was strengthened by a remarkable barbican (pl. 3),
extending the entrance passage by a pair of hornworks and a central
double bank. The ramparts forming this were not of glacis type, but
had vertical faces with upright timbers, the spaces between filled not
with horizontal logs or wattling but with dry-stone walling. There is
thus some reason to suppose that this system of outworks may have
been earlier than the enlargement of the enclosure. On the other hand

Fig. 11   Maiden Castle, evolution. After Sir Mortimer Wheeler.

the west gateway of the enlargement seems to have been of similar design; but the details were not worked out by excavation.

The initial Iron Age settlement, and the extension, can both be attributed to phases of the A culture, but after another half-century B influences appear on the site. The use of the sling, and the consequent introduction or invention of multiple ramparts, are to be attributed to this phase. A second bank and ditch were added round the whole circuit, and a third round the southern side, while the main bank, which had become grass-grown, was almost doubled in size rising to a broad flat top with no breastwork to front or rear. To give stability to this increased height, buried structural revetments were incorporated in the back of the rampart; the highest of these was partly exposed, giving a vertical *inner* face to the upper part of the bank. Much of the stone for these revetments was limestone brought from two miles away, and the material for the bank was largely obtained from a great quarry ditch behind the rampart. This ditch provided a sheltered site for dwellings, and the resulting accumulation of superimposed hut floors provided the archaeologist with valuable information as to the sequence of pottery and other relics. At the eastern entrance a ditch, Y-shaped in plan, its stem extending the bank between the two gateways, prevented a direct approach.

Even with this elaboration, the defences had not reached their final form. In about H 100 or H 50, the ramparts were still further enlarged, a substantial counterscarp bank being added round the whole circuit. It was at this stage that the entrance-works reached their present complexity, better understood from the reconstruction drawing (pl. 4) than from a description. In addition to the elaborate convolutions of the approach, the positioning of platforms for slingers to command their lines of approach is of interest. These defenders would have had no chance of reaching safety should an attack have reached the actual gate, and it seems legitimate to suspect that they were associated with the similarly exposed dwellings in the space just outside the main entrances.

Too little of the interior was cleared to give a detailed picture of its appearance, but at this stage in its development the settlement enclosed would seem to have been typical (see p. 236), the irregularly placed dwellings being interspersed with half-filled refuse pits and grain stores used or disused.

At about H 50, another wave of new influences arrived, Belgic or C, from the south-east. With this change can be associated the introduction not merely of new pottery styles but of coinage. More remarkable and significant was the appearance of 'a new civic discipline', to quote the report. 'The innumerable ... pits, which must have stunk to high heaven, were now everywhere filled up.' And the semi-ruinous rampart was tidied by a thick new coating of earth and provided with a rampart walk open to the front but protected along the back by a fence supported with substantial posts – interpreted by the excavator as corresponding in function to the upper section of vertical revetment which was buried by the added earth, to prevent unauthorized access to the rampart walk from the enclosure.

The security of these great defences must have given the inhabitants confidence to resist the Roman invaders; but they were self-deceived, and the town was one of the twenty which fell to Vespasian in his campaign of the mid-forties of the first century AD. Dramatic evidence of this came from the war cemetery just outside the main eastern gateway, where the remains of thirty-eight bodies were found, ceremonially buried, usually with a pot or other grave goods, in shallow graves cut through the ashes of the adjacent houses. Most of these displayed wounds; several skulls had sword cuts, and in one skeleton a Roman arrowhead was embedded in the backbone. These, no doubt, fell in battle, but others must correspond to subsequent massacre, for several show multiple injuries any one of which would have been fatal: one skull, for example, is marked by nine sword cuts, and there were at least eleven women among the thirty-eight.

After their victory the Romans were content to demolish the main gateways, but to leave the inhabitants, or most of them, in their old home. Not until twenty years later was the place finally abandoned and replaced by Durnovaria, modern Dorchester.

This was not quite the end. In the fourth century, as described earlier (p. 79), a sanctuary was established on the site. We may suspect, but cannot prove, that its priest maintained the worship of the deity who had presided over the Iron Age town from its foundation.

Tre'r Ceiri, in Caernarvonshire, offers a complete contrast to Maiden Castle. It stands 450 metres above sea level, on an exposed peak of Yr Eifl; its walls, of dry stone, still survive in places to their full height; and the footings of the dwellings remain visible. It is probably the best preserved of all the hill towns of southern Britain, and certainly can give a better idea than any other of the original appearance of a place of this kind. Unhappily, its outstanding interest led to extensive excavation before the development of modern techniques, and worse still it is a popular amusement with summer visitors to eviscerate a hut or two, presumably under the impression that in thus spoiling the appearance of the remains and destroying any surviving evidence they are 'doing archaeology'. Nevertheless, in spite of all these disadvantages, the history of the place is now tolerably clear.

The best and easiest approach is from SH 360 437, the end of a minor road north of Llithfaen, rather than by the shorter but very steep climb from the road B 4417; and the most spectacular view is given by a low westerly sun, which picks out the massive walls still standing 4 metres high in places above the dark heather among the screes and rocks. After crossing a level plateau, where ill recorded burials were found by the early excavators, the track winds steeply upwards between low tumbled walls to the ruins of the south-western gateway. The immediate interior displays only rough grass and bilberries, but continuing up the slope towards the summit – with a magnificent view – confused groups of small huts are encountered. The early excavations, by unsupervised labourers clearing through the original floors to the natural subsoil and building up the stones round about, have at least reproduced an approximation to the original height of the hut walls. These extensive clearances also produced relics, exclusively Roman, which indicate that occupation of the place continued into the fourth century AD.

Tre'r Ceiri, then, though often cited as a 'typical' hill-fort, is unique in Britain, for although occupation continued into that period, and later, elsewhere, only at this site is the complete plan of a native town of the Roman period exposed to view.

Careful examination of the remains has shown that the visible arrangement is the result of long evolution. The earliest feature on the hill is the cairn on the summit, a relic of the Bronze Age and unrelated to the fort save by the accident of position. The original enclosure is represented by the main inner wall. In several ways this is notable. Its state of preservation is exceptional, and may be the result of continued use into the Roman period so that it escaped slighting; but, whatever the cause, in places on the north it still retains the original parapet and rampart walk, as well as the sloping ramps by which these were approached. There were five gateways. The two larger are ruinous, but seem to have been unusually narrow. More interesting, perhaps, are the three 'posterns', straight-sided openings less than a metre wide; that on the north retains its lintel, perhaps the only example surviving (though precariously) in a fortress gate in southern Britain. The north-west gate and the north postern gave access to springs. Within the enclosure, the original dwellings seem to have been about twenty round houses (pl. 5), corresponding to a population of about a hundred persons.

So far, apart from being set unusually high, the hill-fort was fairly typical for the region; the present exceptional character is the result of its continued occupation during the Roman period. The changes which followed are described as if they all took place at the same time, for their sequence cannot be worked out, but in fact they may have been spread out over three centuries.

The most striking development was the alteration in the shape of the dwellings and the great increase in their number (pl. 1). In plan, they were mostly irregular or roughly rectangular, less than half the area of the earlier round houses; typologically, they could have evolved out of the D-shaped plan resulting from the subdivision of the latter. Instead of a mere score there were at least 150, so even allowing fewer inhabitants to the smaller compartments the population must have been trebled or quadrupled. The defences were reinforced by a long stretch of outer wall on the north, and by shorter lengths on each side of the western approach. Where the north wall meets the terraced track leading from the north-west gateway to the spring, an unusual out-turned gateway was built, the northern jamb crossing the older trackway, which was diverted. All round the skirts of the hill, too, except on its steepest parts, little amoeboid enclosures were constructed. Their interiors, now mostly bare scree or rubble, were formed into level terraces behind fairly well built retaining walls.

Even if this analysis of its structural development is accepted as satisfactory, this remarkable settlement still poses one problem for solution. Its general character has every appearance of a small town, permanently occupied, and the little terraced enclosures are hardly explicable save as plots for some form of cultivation. Yet today the place is decidedly inhospitable even on many days in summer, and to live there throughout the year, or to cultivate even the hardiest crop, would seem unthinkable. It seems necessary to postulate some climatic change, possibly quite small and local; this need not have been greater than the variation which may occur now, for although on many August days the hill top may be enveloped in a bitterly cold mist, by contrast one may experience warm and almost idyllic sunshine in mid-winter.

On Traprain Law (fig. 12, pl. 6), in East Lothian, the visible remains are relatively unimpressive, but the story of its occupation extends almost unbroken from the end of the Bronze Age into the early Christian period. A campaign of excavation early in this century, though crude by modern standards, demonstrated beyond doubt that the surface of this hill conceals a rich mass of information for more than a millennium of the archaeology and early history of the lowlands and northern England.

At the time of writing, this unique document is being steadily destroyed unread, for the rock on which it stands yields profit if sold for road-making. If Britain is so poverty-stricken, in outlook even if not in reality, that this inexcusable destruction cannot be stopped, it should at least be preceded by *total* scientific excavation of the area to be dug away. Areas not under threat could, and indeed should, be left alone except for limited investigations to establish the sequence of events; for excavation techniques are steadily improving, and this is a particularly difficult site.

The area cleared on the western slopes during the period 1914 to 1923 covered some 5,000 square metres, and produced a mass of material, but neither the method of excavation nor its recording were of the high standard such a site deserves, and the separate reports have never been combined to provide a definitive final account. These researches were supplemented by careful though very limited investigations in 1939 and 1947, but it remained for Mr Feachem, then on the staff of the Royal Commission on Ancient and Historical Monuments in Scotland, to prepare an accurate survey and to work out the probable development of the site (which is followed here). At the same time, Miss Elizabeth Burley (now Mrs E. Fowler) published a full study of the metalwork – over six hundred items. The glass objects and the mass of pottery have not yet been adequately described.

Five systems of defences can be distinguished on the hill, with possible faint traces of one yet earlier phase. All except the latest rampart are very ruinous, though the penultimate structure is still fairly well defined.

The doubtful earliest phase is represented by intermittent lengths of a slight scarp and lines of stones following the main axis of the hill. If this does correspond to the first defensive line, it protected an area of about 4 hectares.

The next phase, the earliest which can be recognized with certainty, was identified by Mr S. Cruden in 1939. The highest part of the hill, covering about 8 hectares, was enclosed by a rampart in the form of a terrace with an external revetment of stone. Only very small excavations have been made in this enclosure, so nothing reliable can be said as to its absolute date.

Fig. 12   Traprain Law. After R. W. Feachem.

In the second (certain) phase, a similar rampart was built to protect the lower slopes of the hill to the west, increasing the enclosed area to 12 hectares. Almost all the excavations of 1914–21 were within this area, but the discoveries cannot be related directly to the ramparts. Their significance is discussed below.

The next stage can be dated to some time within the first century AD, and the town, as it may fairly be called, now reached its greatest extent, 16 hectares. The rampart, again, was a revetted terrace, and excavation has shown that it was repaired or rebuilt in about AD 300. This was not the last of the defences, for later still a wall, 3·5 metres thick, of turf faced on both sides with stone, was built on about the same line as the second certain rampart, reducing the area once again to 12 hectares. There were thus five certain periods of rampart-building (referred to below as first to fifth without qualification) and one doubtful; the third and fourth can be dated to some time within the first century AD, and to about AD 300 respectively, and the fifth is probably post-Roman. The first and second are pre-Roman. The excavations of 1914–21 were outside the lines of the first rampart (and of the doubtful earlier one) but within all the others. The objects from these excavations which have been dated fall into three groups: the Late Bronze Age, say H 700–500; first century BC to second century AD, the last exactly dated object in this group being a coin assigned to AD 155; and third century AD to the end of the Roman period, the earliest and latest coins being of AD 253 and 408 respectively. There is a tradition of a monastery founded on the site by St Monenna in about AD 500, and a massive silver chain of about the sixth to eighth century AD was found on the hill.

Leaving aside accepted views as to the probable dates of hill-fort building, this material can be combined into a self-consistent account. The undated fifth rampart is correlated with the early Christian occupation indicated by tradition but by no relics except the silver chain. The fourth rampart, built about AD 300, corresponds satisfactorily with the occupation indicated by coins from 253 to AD 408, and other late metalwork. Similarly, some of the objects assigned to the period of the first century BC to the second century AD, with the run of coins ending at AD 155, can be related to the third rampart, built some time in the first century AD.

The Late Bronze Age objects were found within the line of the second phase rampart, but outside that of the first phase. Logically, therefore, it would seem reasonable to regard the second rampart as of the Late Bronze Age, and the first as still earlier, but even though recent work as at Ivinghoe and Dinorben would now make one period of fortification at such an early date seem plausible it is still difficult to accept two. It seems better, at least for the present, to associate the earliest material with the first rampart, as an extramural deposit. The second rampart may then be assigned to the beginning of the main pre-Roman occupation.

Pending further investigation, we cannot tell whether the people living on the hill when the Romans arrived were the direct descendants of those who utilized all the Late Bronze Age material found there, or whether there was renewed occupation in the first century BC, after a period of abandonment. The relics seem to demonstrate that in this region the Romans were welcomed. The town seems to have prospered, and the inhabitants obtained quite a lot of metal objects and pottery from the new arrivals, while continuing to make their own. They seem to have lived in round houses, but only one really satisfactory plan was recovered. This was about 6 metres in diameter, enclosed by a massive wall over 2 metres thick, of turf or cob on a foundation of slabs; there was a central hearth.

Something drastic happened soon after the middle of the second century, but again the story must remain obscure pending further excavation; tentatively, it seems likely that the town was abandoned for a generation. The Romans experienced a military setback at about this time, and withdrew from Scotland, and their friends at Traprain may also have suffered. When the place was re-occupied, it stood outside the area of direct Roman control, but within an allied client kingdom, or protectorate. Once again Roman objects are plentiful, and remain so until at least the beginning of the fifth century. One particularly notable find was a stylus, implying that some inhabitants could write.

The latest buildings seem to have had walls of mixed earth and stone, and the lines of rubble debris recorded by the excavators thus give some idea of the arrangement of the town in its final state. The dwellings were roughly rectangular, with rounded corners, the walls being 1·5 to 2 metres thick, sometimes more. Most houses consisted of a single fairly large compartment, 5 or 6 metres wide and of about twice that length; one, not fully uncovered, was more than 23 metres long. They were thus very much more commodious than the houses at Tre'r Ceiri. Almost all contained a large hearth near the middle of the floor, and some had small compartments opening off the main room. The area excavated was traversed by a road 2·5 to 3 metres wide, with cart ruts; its continuation in each direction remains visible. The houses mostly stood close together along this, but near the middle of the area cleared they were set back so as to form an irregular square about 20 metres across, which the line of the road crossed diagonally. The detail recorded does not permit an attempt at reconstruction, but they can be visualized as resembling the poorest type of cottage which still survived until recently in the remoter parts of Britain: windowless, with low walls of mud on a boulder foundation; there would be no chimney, and such peat smoke as could not escape by the doorway would seep out through the heavy rough thatch.

Only about a dozen houses were excavated, and Mr Feachem's plan shows some fifty or more platforms which could have carried others, so the richer inhabitants may have had more impressive dwellings. One man, at least, seems to have hoped to become more prosperous, for beneath the floor of one of the compartments south of the square was a large hoard of late Roman silver, evidently from its damaged condition – some vessels had been halved – representing one share of the loot from a successful raid. This find is often cited as evidence that the town was deserted, but its date falls within the limits of the coin sequence, and there would have been no problem in bringing it to the house, perhaps disguised as a sack of straw.

The story of St Monenna remains as yet unsupported by archaeology, but contains nothing inherently unlikely. If accepted, it implies that Traprain, under the name Dunpeldur, was still a flourishing small town at the beginning of the sixth century, and that somewhere on the hill top one of the earliest Christian churches in Britain awaits discovery – unless it has already been destroyed for road-metalling.

Fig. 13   Croft Ambrey. After S. C. Stanford.

Croft Ambrey (fig. 13) has been the site of one of the most important excavations in Britain. The investigation not only made it possible to recognize, for the first time, a new 'culture' in western England, but provided a more convincingly reliable chronology than any established hitherto, by considering the probable duration of the successive phases in the reconstructions which took place in the gateways; the dating is based on a thirty-year life for the posts, with controls provided by radiocarbon. The history of the site can therefore be set out in considerable detail, with fairly reliable absolute dates. The phases, in this account, follow those of the excavation report.

The position chosen was a long narrow hill, with a very abrupt scarp on the north and gentler, though still steep, slopes on the other sides. On the summit of this hill, in about 550 BC, a small dump rampart and ditch were built to protect an enclosure of 2·2 hectares. The interior was closely set with small four-post buildings regularly spaced along streets. This house pattern continued with little change throughout the six centuries of the hill-fort's life. It is discussed further below. The gateway in this first phase was a simple double portal, formed by three large posts. It was entirely rebuilt to the same design twice, and the posts were renewed twice more, giving a sequence of five successive sets of posts (covering phases one to three). No pottery, and very few relics of any kind, survived from the occupation of this earlier fort.

In the next stage (pl. 7), about 390 BC, a new and massive rampart was built, following a line mostly outside the old one. Although large, it was of simple design, being a bank with a glacis-type front running smoothly down into its single ditch. The width overall was 28 metres, and the vertical height 12 metres; the crest carried a timber breastwork. The ditch was not big enough to supply all the material for the bank, so a large quarry ditch was dug out. The filling of this quarry ditch provided a valuable series of stratified layers.

This rampart style remained unaltered for some 290 years (phases four to six), but there were changes in the design of the gateways during that time; these were best worked out at the south-west entrance. Initially (phase four) this gateway was very similar to that of the plateau camp, with a passageway nearly 7 metres wide leading to a double portal. The rampart ends were only slightly thickened, giving a passage about 5 metres long. With reconstructions, this type of gate lasted about sixty years.

In about 330 BC, the entrance was drastically replanned and strengthened (phase five). The width of the passage was almost halved, to 4 metres, and the broad double portal replaced by a single one. The gate passage was lengthened, and a pair of rectangular guard rooms provided. Sandstone, brought from the foot of the hill, was used for the lower courses of walling in this phase. The gate posts were joined by a rubble-filled trench across the entrance passage, and it seems likely, as the excavator suggests, that the opening may have been closed, in emergencies, by a temporary palisade set up in this – whether as a reinforcement to a hung gate or as an alternative cannot be decided.

This phase lasted until about 260 BC, when the system of guard rooms was given up, the gate being set at the inner end of a straight-sided passage. There was no evidence for a bridge. There were six replacements of the posts during this phase, which is estimated to have lasted some 190 years, to about 70 BC.

In the last phase (seven) the gateway arrangements were similar, save that a bridge was added across the passage in front of the gate. To this phase, also, there can probably be attributed the second bank and ditch formed outside the main bank. There was no further alteration, and the effective occupation of the hill-fort ended with the arrival of the Romans in AD 48.

All the above refers to the main enclosure. Outside this there is a relatively weak annexe, of 4·8 hectares. This was not extensively investigated, for one primary objective of the work was to throw light on the history of the adjacent hill-forts also, and annexes are rare among them; but sufficient was done to show that the lines of close-set rectangular buildings did not occur in it. Nevertheless, the annexe did contain a remarkable sacred site, which in its earliest phases consisted of a levelled terrace cut into the hillside. About AD 150 this was covered by a mound 11·6 metres square and up to 1·5 metres high, with a rough dry-stone revetment on three sides. The religious ceremonies, whatever they may have been, left much charcoal, ash and burned bone, and many fragments of broken pottery. The latest datable sherd was of the third or fourth century.

As mentioned earlier, the occupants of the first enclosure lived in little rectangular huts ranging from 2·4 by 1·8 metres to 3·6 metres square. Some essentially similar buildings were storehouses or granaries, which could be distinguished merely by such accidents as the preservation of carbonized grain. In addition to the contrast in shape and size, as compared to the dwellings in such forts as Garn Boduan or Hod Hill, there was an equally sharp contrast in arrangement, for the buildings were regularly set out in streets. Moreover, evidence was found that they had been repeatedly rebuilt on the same site; sometimes as many as six renewals of the uprights could be detected.

This barrack-like settlement differs so radically from the haphazard round house pattern that it seems impossible to avoid the conclusion that the origins of the Croft Ambrey settlers must be sought outside Britain, although Croft Ambrey itself was probably the work of descendants of the original invaders.

Another interesting result of this work is the evidence for the development of quite an extensive system of trade. In phases one to three, the plateau camp, pottery is almost absent; in later phases it becomes plentiful, and can be proved (by its mineral content) to derive from potters working in the Malvern Hills region, 30 kilometres away; the infrequency of the supply is emphasized by the discovery of a large proportion of potsherds with indications of repair by iron rivets.

Bibliography

This is not intended to be complete. Its object is to give the main sources used, and these will provide a foundation for anyone who wishes to go into the subject more deeply. Papers which deal primarily with particular sites but which also contain material of wider relevance are indicated by the hill-fort name, under which (in the gazetteer) the reference is given.

GENERAL WORKS

These are also referred to in some sections relating to separate chapters, and in the gazetteer, using the abbreviations indicated.

H F N F   Sir Mortimer Wheeler and K. M. Richardson, *Hill-forts of Northern France*, Research Report XIX, Society of Antiquaries of London (1957). Important for study of continental origins.

I A H F   D. Hill and M. Jesson (eds), *The Iron Age and its Hill-forts*, Univ. of Southampton Monograph 1 (Southampton, 1971).

I A Map   *Map of Southern Britain in the Iron Age* with introduction (Ordnance Survey, 1962). A corresponding map for northern Britain is in preparation.

I A N B   A. L. F. Rivet (ed.), *The Iron Age in Northern Britain* (Edinburgh, 1966).

P I A S B   S. S. Frere (ed.), *Problems of the Iron Age in Southern Britain*, Institute of Archaeology Occasional Paper 11 (Univ. of London, *c*. 1958).

P P   F. T. Wainwright (ed.), *Problem of the Picts* (Nelson, 1955), especially R. W. Feachem (ch. III) on fortifications.

Note also the following abbreviations: *Ant. J, Antiquaries Journal* *Arch. J, Archaeological Journal Preh. Scot*, R. W. Feachem, *Prehistoric Scotland* (Batsford 1963).

An important book which will provide the long needed background to the British Iron Age has been announced while this work was in its final stages of preparation: B. Cunliffe, *Iron Age Communities in Britain* (Archaeology of Britain series, Routledge, 1974).

INDIVIDUAL CHAPTERS

1 Names. The basic sources for England are the various publications of the English Place Name Society, and for Scotland W. J. Watson, *Celtic Place Names of Scotland* (Edinburgh, 1926). Names mentioned in classical sources, and thus often preserving the pre-Roman form, are discussed by I. A. Richmond, O. G. S. Crawford and I. Williams in 'The British Section of the Ravenna Cosmography', *Archaeologia* XCIII (1949), pp. 1–50, and by K. Jackson, 'Romano-British Names in the Antonine Itinerary', *Britannia* I (1970), pp. 68–82.

2 Modern Research. Most modern research appears in reports on separate hill-forts (see gazetteer) or among the more recent of the county surveys (pp. 107–11). For general works see *I A H F*, *I A N B* and *P I A S B*. Some attempts at theoretical or numerical analysis are given in *I A H F*, pp. 59–64, 114–24.

3 The Background. For the Hawkes–Piggott framework see C. F. C. Hawkes, *P I A S B*, pp. 1–16, and S. Piggott, *I A N B*, pp. 1–15. Revised evidence for date: in the Welsh Marches, S. C. Stanford in *I A H F*, pp. 42–3; also under Credenhill, Croft Ambrey, and H. N. Savory under Dinorben; in Scotland, E. W. MacKie, *Antiquity* XLII (1969), pp. 15–26.

For Celtic life in general: T. G. E. Powell, *The Celts* (Thames and Hudson, London, 1958); J. Filip, *Celtic Civilization and its Heritage* (English trans. by R. F. Samsour, Prague, 1962); S. Piggott, *Ancient Europe* (Edinburgh, 1965), pp. 168 ff. (chs 5 and 6). A. Ross, *Everyday Life of the Pagan Celts* (Batsford 1970).

Economics: in *I A H F*, B. Cunliffe (cultural environment) pp. 53–9; R. Bradley (economic change) pp. 71–83; J. Collis (markets and money) pp. 97–103; also R. Bradley, 'Stock Raising and the Origins of the Hill-Fort on the South Downs', *Ant. J.* LI (1971), pp. 8–29.

4 Function. See generally under places named in chapter, also *I A H F*, as under chs 2 and 3. For size distribution see under Croft Ambrey and (for Wales) A. H. A. Hogg in *Prehistoric Man in Wales and the West* (ed. F. Lynch and C. Burgess, Adams and Dart, Bath, 1972), pp. 293–307. On function (and population) in the Welsh Marches, S. C. Stanford, *ibid.*, pp. 307–20. See also under ch. 5.

5 Distribution and Regional Types. The south-western wide-spaced multivallate type: A. Fox in *P I A S B*, pp. 35 ff., and *Arch. J.* CIX (1952), pp. 1–22.

Scottish and Northumbrian forts: R. W. Feachem, in *I A N B*, pp. 59–88, and G. Jobey, *ibid.*, pp. 89–109.

Territories: J. F. Dyer, 'Dray's Ditches, Bedfordshire, and E.I.A. Territorial Boundaries in the E. Chilterns', *Ant. J.* XLI (1961), pp. 32–43.

For discussion of a particular region, see *The Iron Age in the Irish Sea Province* (ed. C. Thomas, CBA, London, 1972), especially A. H. A. Hogg (pp. 11–24), S. C. Stanford (pp. 25–36) and (summing up) L. Alcock (pp. 99–111).

6 Origins, Attack and Defence. General discussion with numerous references: C. F. C. Hawkes in *I A H F*, pp. 5–18. See also S. Piggott, *Ancient Europe* as under ch. 3.

Chevaux-de-frise: P. Harbison, 'Wooden and Stone *C.-de-f.* in Central and Western Europe', *Proc. Preh. Soc.* XXXVII (1971), pp. 195–225. This valuable paper, in conjunction with other refs given in it, makes *all* the evidence readily available.

Caesar's descriptions of warfare in Gaul and Britain: complete discussion with summaries and corrections of some current mistranslations, A. L. F. Rivet in *I A H F*, pp. 189–202.

7 Building the Hill Fort. R. W. Feachem's discussion of unfinished hill forts (in *I A H F*, pp. 19–39) is of primary importance. See also A. L. F. Rivet in *P I A S B*, pp. 29–34, and under Ladle Hill, Bindon Hill, Harding's Down and Overton Down.

8 The Ramparts. Palisaded enclosures: R. W. Feachem in *I A N B*, pp. 59–65; A. Ritchie, 'Palisaded Sites in N. Britain', *Scottish Arch. Forum* (1970), pp. 48–68.

Quarry ditches: A. L. F. Rivet in *P I A S B*, pp. 29–34.

Galleried duns, etc.: see under Clickhimin.

Timber lacing: M. A. Cotton, 'British Camps with Timber-laced Ramparts', *Arch. J.* CXI (1954), pp. 26–105; and on *muri gallici*, *H F N F*, pp. 159–225.

Satellite forts: J. Forde-Johnston, 'Earls Hill Pontesbury and Related Hill-forts', *Arch. J.* CXIX (1962), pp. 66–91.

9 The Gateways. See generally under places named.

Chronology (in Welsh Marches): S. C. Stanford in *I A H F*, pp. 42–5.

10 The Interior. See under places named. Also (for nature of post settings) A. Ellison and P. Drewett, 'Pits and Post-holes in the British Early Iron Age', *Proc. Preh. Soc.* XXXVII, 1 (1971), pp. 183–94.

11 The Romans and After. Distribution of forts in the south, defended and not defended against Roman attack: B. Cunliffe in *I A H F*, p. 67.

Later fortifications: R. W. Feachem in *P P*, pp. 66–86 and (modifying earlier views) in *I A N B*, pp. 82–5. Also R. B. K. Stevenson, *Proc. Soc. Ant. Scot.* LXXXIII (1948–9), pp. 186–97. And see under Dinas Emrys, Dunadd, Dundurn and Ruberslaw.

GENERAL TOPOGRAPHICAL INFORMATION

The following works include, among other material, useful summary descriptions of many hill-forts.

N. Thomas, *A Guide to Prehistoric England* (Batsford, London, 1960).

R. W. Feachem, *Prehistoric Scotland* (Batsford, London, 1963).

C. H. Houlder, *Wales, an Archaeological Guide* (Faber and Faber, London, forthcoming).

J. Dyer, *Southern England, an Archaeological Guide* (Faber and Faber, London, 1973).

For most British counties there are more or less complete accounts of the hill-forts, either in the relevant volume of the *Victoria County History* (*V C H*) or in a county *Inventory* (*Inv.*) published by Her Majesty's Stationery Office for one of the three Royal Commissions on Ancient and Historical Monuments, for England, Scotland or Wales and Monmouthshire, as appropriate. Most of these publications are fully illustrated with plans unless otherwise noted; but allowances must be made for the difference in standards between (say) 1908 and 1968. In the following list the termination 'shire' is usually omitted for brevity.

ENGLAND

Two important recent publications deal with the Iron Age in full, not hill-forts only, for regions covering parts of several counties. These are D. W. Harding, *The Iron Age in the Upper Thames Basin* (Oxford, 1972), and C. Saunders, 'The Pre-Belgic Iron Age in the Central and Western Chilterns', *Arch. J.* CXXVIII (1971), pp. 1–30. Both are concerned with parts of Berks. Bucks. and Oxford.

Bedford	*V C H* I (1904), pp. 267 ff.
Berks.	*V C H* I (1906), pp. 251 ff., supplemented by M. A. Cotton, *Berks. Arch. J.* LX (1962), pp. 30–52 (no plans). And see above before list of counties.
Bucks.	*Inv.*, 2 vols (1912–13), supersedes *V C H* II (1908), pp. 21 ff. And see above before list of counties.
Cambridgeshire	Inventories: West, 1968; North-east 1972; remainder forthcoming.
Cheshire	J. Forde-Johnston, *Trans. Lancs. and Cheshire Arch. Soc.* LXXII (1962), pp. 9–46.
Cornwall	*V C H* I (1906), pp. 451 ff. (not as complete as most *V C H*), supplemented, for cliff castles, by M. A. Cotton, *West Cornwall Field Club* II, 3 (1958–9), pp. 113 ff. (no plans).
Cumberland	*V C H* I (1901), p. 232. Map only, no descriptions or plans. Refs with no descriptions or plans: *Archaeologia* LIII (1893), pp. 485–538.
Derby	*V C H* I (1905), pp. 357 ff.
Devon	*V C H* I (1906), pp. 573 ff. Also C. Whybrow, *Proc. Devon Arch. Soc. No. 25* (1967), pp. 1–18. Discussion, with plans, of nine forts in north-west of county.
Dorset	*Inv.*, 3 vols in 6 parts, 1952–70.
Durham	*V C H* I (1905), pp. 343 ff.
Essex	*Inv.*, 4 vols (1916–23), superseding *V C H* I (1903), 275 ff.
Gloucester	No adequate account of county's hill-forts.
Hants.	J. P. Williams Freeman, *Field Archaeology as Illustrated by Hampshire* (London, 1915). An excellent work, fully illustrated with plans.

Hereford   *Inv.*, 3 vols (1931–4), superseding *V C H* I
                  (1908), pp. 199 ff.
Herts.   *Inv.* (1910), superseding *V C H* II (1908), pp.
                  103 ff.
Hunts.   *Inv.* (1926); also *V C H* I (1926), pp. 281 ff.
Kent   *V C H* I (1908), pp. 389 ff.
Lancs.   J. Forde-Johnston as for Cheshire; also *V C H* II
                  (1966), pp. 507 ff.
Leicester   *V C H* I (1907), pp. 243 ff.
Lincoln   C. W. Phillips, *Arch. J.* XCI (1934), pp. 101–2,
                  gives a brief account of the few hill-forts in the
                  county. One air photo but no plans.
Middlesex   *Inv.* (1937); but county contains no hill-forts.
Norfolk   R. R. Clarke, 'Iron Age in Norfolk and Suffolk',
                  Arch. J. XCVI (1939), pp. 48–9, gives a brief
                  account of the few hill forts, with small-scale
                  plans.
Northants.   *V C H* II (1906), pp. 397 ff.
Northumberland   G. Jobey, *Arch. Aeliana* 4 ser XLIII (1965), pp.
                  21–64.
Nottingham   B. B. Simmons, *Trans. Thoroton Soc.* LXVII
                  (1963), pp. 9–20, describing the five known forts,
                  with plans. Largely supersedes *V C H* I (1906),
                  pp. 289 ff.
Oxford   No general account of hill-forts, but see above
                  before list of counties.
Rutland   *V C H* I (1908), pp. 107 ff., but no hill-forts
                  recorded.
Shropshire   *V C H* I (1908), pp. 351 ff.
Somerset   *V C H* II (1911), pp. 467 ff.
Staffs.   *V C H* I (1908), pp. 331 ff.
Suffolk   *V C H* I (1911), pp. 583 ff., and see R. R. Clarke
                  as for Norfolk
Surrey   *V C H* IV (1912), pp. 379 ff.
Sussex   *V C H* I (1905), pp. 453 ff.
Warwick   *V C H* I (1904), pp. 345 ff.
Westmoreland   *Inv.* (1936).
Wilts.   The collection of plans in R. Colt Hoare, *Ancient
                  Wiltshire* I (1812), has now been supplemented
                  and partly superseded by *V.C H* I, pt 1 (1957)

for bibliography, pt 2 (1974) for valuable discussion by Professor Cunliffe with three aerial views and eleven new plans (to various irrational scales).

Worcester   *V C H* I (1901), pp. 184 ff.; inferior to other *V C H* volumes.

Yorks   *V C H* II (1912), pp. 1 ff.

SCOTLAND (mainland only)

Although several counties have not been treated in detail the whole country has been at least partly covered by D. Christison, *Ancient Earthworks and Camps of Scotland* (Edinburgh, 1898).

Aberdeen   No separate account.

Angus   D. Christison, *Proc. Soc. Ant. Scot.* XXXIV (1899–1900), pp. 43 ff.

Argyll   D. Christison, *Proc. Soc. Ant. Scot.* XXIII (1888–9), pp. 368 ff. (NW); *ibid.* XXXVIII (1903–4), pp. 205 ff. (Mid). The latter is supplemented and partly superseded by M. Campbell and M. L. S. Sandeman, *ibid.* XCV (1961–2), pp. 39–60, with good summary descriptions and full references but no plans. Also *Inv.* for Kintyre (Argyll vol. I, HMSO, 1971).

Ayr   D. Christison, *Proc. Soc. Ant. Scot.* XXVII (1892–3), pp. 381 ff.

Banff   No account.

Berwick   *Inv.* (2nd edn 1915).

Caithness   *Inv.* (1911).

Clackmannan   See *Fife Inv.*

Dumfries   *Inv.* (1920).

Dumbarton   No account.

Fife   *Inv.* with Kinross and Clackmannan (1933).

Inverness   No account of any value.

Kincardine   D. Christison, *Proc. Soc. Ant. Scot.* XXXIV (1899–1900), pp. 43 ff.

Kinross   See *Fife Inv.*

Kirkcudbright   *Inv.* (1914).
Lanark   D. Christison, *Proc. Soc. Ant. Scot.* XXIV
                         (1889–90), pp. 281–352 (Upper Ward
                         only).
Lothian, East   *Inv.* (1924).
Lothian, Mid and West   *Inv.* (1929).
Moray   No account.
Nairn   No account.
Peebles   *Inv.*, 2 vols (1967).
Perth   D. Christison, *Proc. Soc. Ant. Scot.*
                         XXXIV (1899–1900), pp. 43 ff.
Renfrew   No account.
Ross and Cromarty   No account.
Roxburgh   *Inv.*, 2 vols (1956).
Selkirk   *Inv.* (1957).
Stirling   *Inv.*, 2 vols (1963).
Sutherland   *Inv.* (1911).
Wigtown   *Inv.* (1912).

WALES

Anglesey   *Inv.* (1937, reprinted 1970).
Brecknock   H. N. Savory, *Bulletin of Board of Celtic Studies*
                XIV.1 (Nov. 1950), pp. 69 ff. Addenda, XV.3 (Nov.
                1953), pp. 230 ff. List with reference and discussion
                but little detail and no plans. Further discussion with
                small-scale plans, *Brycheiniog* I (1954), pp. 119–25.
Caernarvon   *Inv.*, 3 vols (1956–64).
Cardigan   A. H. A. Hogg, *Bulletin of Board of Celtic Studies*
                XIX.4 (May 1962), pp. 354 ff. (List as for
                Brecknock.)
Carmarthen   *Inv.* (1917) and *County History* vol. I (1935), pp.
                70–90, contain some material but greatly need
                revision. They are partly supplemented by H. N.
                Savory, *Bulletin of Board of Celtic Studies* XVI.1
                (Nov. 1954). (List as for Brecknock.)
Denbigh   *Inv.* (1914) requires revision and largely superseded
                by Ellis Davies, *Prehistoric and Roman Remains of
                Denbs.* (Cardiff, 1929).
Flint   *Inv.* (1912) requires revision and largely superseded

	by Ellis Davies, *Prehistoric and Roman Remains of Flints*. (1949).
Glamorgan	*Inv.* forthcoming. Pending publication see H. N. Savory, *Bulletin of Board of Celtic Studies* XIII.3 (Nov. 1949), pp. 152 ff. Addenda XV.3 (Nov. 1953), pp. 229 ff. (List as for Brecknock.)
Merioneth	*County History*, Vol. I (Dolgellau, 1967). Very fully illustrated with good plans.
Monmouth	H. N. Savory, *Bulletin of Board of Celtic Studies* XIII.4 (May 1950), pp. 231 ff. Addenda XV.3 (Nov. 1953), pp. 229 ff. (List as for Brecknock.)
Montgomery	*Inv.* (1911) requires revision.
Pembroke	*Inv.* (1925) requires revision, and supplemented by D. W. Crossley, *Bulletin of Board of Celtic Studies* XX (May 1963), pp. 171 ff. (List as for Brecknock.)
Radnor	*Inv.* (1913) requires revision, and supplemented by H. N. Savory, *Bulletin of Board of Celtic Studies* XV.1 (Nov. 1952), pp. 73 ff. (List as for Brecknock.)

ADDENDUM

Two important works have been announced while this book was in page proof:

J. Forde-Johnston, *Hill-forts of the Iron Age in England and Wales: a survey of the surface evidence* (Liverpool University Press, 1975). This is a detailed scientific study, the scope of which is indicated by the title.

D. W. Harding (Editor), *Hill-forts: Later Prehistoric Earthworks in Britain and Ireland* (Academic Press, 1975). This contains sixteen articles, including detailed reports on Almondbury, Mam Tor, Ravensburgh and Salmonsbury; and re-assessments of the evidence from St Catherine's Hill and Traprain Law.

Gazetteer

This has two main objectives: to describe a representative sample; and to give fuller details, including the main references, for all those which are mentioned in the text, so as to avoid interruption by footnotes or descriptions which may be irrelevant in the immediate context. The arrangement is strictly alphabetical, so it provides an index to all places named.

Selection, out of the 2,500 or so hill-forts on the British mainland, proved difficult; it is hoped that an explanation of the principles adopted may mitigate readers' annoyance at discovering the omission of places which they regard as of particular interest or importance.

The original plan was to include at least one fort, if such existed, in each quarter of every 100-kilometre square of the National Grid, together with every excavated site. The list proved impossibly long, and had to be cut drastically. In doing this, major weight has been given to the need to keep a fairly even distribution. One of the chief faults of British archaeology is its localized bias, especially towards the south and east, and if full attention had been paid to the classic sites of the southern chalklands the north and west would have been badly under-represented. It is for this reason that many impressive structures have been left out in favour of such places as Am Baghan Burblach or Ashie Moor; others, though retained, have been given briefer treatment than they deserve. Further, for reasons given earlier, hill-forts recently or currently under excavation, and for which a report is pending, have in general been excluded; at a few the interim reports have yielded information of such interest that some mention is unavoidable. When, as at Craig Phadrig, work has begun since the text was drafted, the entry has usually been retained essentially unaltered.

The British forts described are shown on the three maps (figs 14–16) indexed by 100-kilometre squares. The descriptions, including foreign sites, are arranged in strict alphabetical order. Each entry gives the name, followed by the figure reference if any, then the historic county, the National Grid reference, and the approximate average height in metres above ordnance datum. The page references which follow indicate where there is further information about the site; mere mentions of the name are not indexed. The sheet numbers of the 1-inch OS map and of its successor the 1/50000 are given in the index to the gazetteer (pp. 114–21).

The accompanying text summarizes the main features of the hill-fort, but does not attempt either a minutely detailed description of the remains or a discussion of the various alternative interpretations which are usually possible. Only the most important references are given in the bibliographical notes.

The plans have been derived from many different sources (see p. vi) and have been redrawn to a standard set of scales and conventions (fig. 17). The need to redraw has often been a matter for regret, for some of the originals are works of art; but it is hoped that any aesthetic loss will be counterbalanced by the advantages of uniformity. Since the chief object is to illustrate the principles used in the design of hill-forts, an attempt to show the exact form of the present ruins could often be confusing rather than helpful, and a really definitive representation would require a much larger scale than is possible here. The plans are therefore essentially diagrammatic. Modern features are usually omitted and the effects of recent disturbances eliminated where this can be done with fair certainty. In the appended acknowledgements, 'after' implies a direct copy of the outline, and 'based on' indicates that there have been some modifications, generally from an examination of the remains by the writer. When the scale is shown as 'approximate' the plan is usually a sketch from a pace-and-prismatic survey, or one of similar accuracy.

Almost all the hill-forts included here are on private land, and although most can be reached without much difficulty *in general the public has no legal right of access*. Where there is any doubt, permission should be sought. Further, the visitor is most strongly urged not to disturb the remains *in any way*. This is not merely because to do so might well render him liable to a fine or even imprisonment under the laws protecting national monuments, but because such activities hasten the decay of the structures and may destroy important evidence.

For a few sites, important new information has been published very recently. This has been incorporated in the gazetteer, but no alteration has been made elsewhere. There may therefore be occasional discrepancies, as for example in the discussion of the original name of Almondbury.

Index to Gazetteer

NT	3	Dunsapie	282 731	62	66
	4	Eildon Hill North	555 328	70	73
	5	Ruberslaw	580 155	70	73
	6	Traprain Law	581 746	63	67
	7	Bonchester Hill	595 117	70	73
	8	Woden Law	768 125	70	80
	9	Edinshall	772 603	63	67
	10	Hownam Rings	790 194	70	74
	11	Camp Tops, Morebattle	860 180	70	74
	12	Yeavering Bell	928 293	71	74
NU	1	The Ringses, Doddington Moor	014 327	71	75
NW	1	Kemp's Walk	975 598	79	82
NX	1	Mull of Galloway	143 307	79	82
	2	Barsalloch Point	347 413	79	82
NY	1	Burnswark	185 785	75	78
	2	Carrock Fell	342 336	83	90
NZ	1	Lordenshaws	054 993	71	81
	2	Stanwick	180 115	85	92
	3	Maiden Castle, Durham	283 417	85	88
	4	Eston Nab	568 183	86	93
SD	1	Skelmore Heads	274 751	88	96
	2	Ingleborough	741 747	90	98
SE	1	Almondbury	152 140	102	110
	2	Grimthorpe	816 535	98	106
	3	Staple Howe	898 749	93	100
SH	1	Castell Odo	187 284	115	123
	2	Caer y Twr	219 829	106	114
	3	Dinllaen	275 416	115	123
	4	Carn Fadrun	280 352	115	123
	5	Garn Boduan	310 393	115	123
	6	Tre'r Ceiri	373 446	115	123
	7	Dinlle	437 563	115	123
	8	Dinorwig	550 653	107	115
	9	Dinas Emrys	606 492	107	115
	10	Pen-y-Gaer, Llanbedr-y-Cennin	750 693	107	115
	11	Conway Mountain	760 778	107	115
	12	Caer Caradog	968 479	108	116
	13	Dinorben	968 757	108	116

SJ	1	Moel Hiraddug	063	785	108	116
	2	Foel Fenlli	163	601	108	116
	3	Llanymynech Hill	265	220	117	126
	4	Old Oswestry	296	310	118	126
	5	Maiden Castle, Bickerton	498	528	109	117
	6	The Wrekin	629	082	118	127
SK	1	Mam Tor	128	838	111	110
	2	Carlwark	260	815	111	110
	3	Caesar's Camp, Scholes Coppice	395	952	103	110
	4	Breedon-on-the-Hill	406	234	121	129
	5	Honington	954	423	113	130
SM	1	St David's Head	722	279	138	157
	2	Walesland Rath	912	170	138	157
SN	1	Moel Trigarn	158	336	139	145
	2	Trelissey	175	078	152	158
	3	Castell Nadolig	298	504	139	145
	4	Pen Dinas, Aberystwyth	584	804	127	135
SO	1	Ffridd Faldwyn	217	969	128	161
	2	Caer Caradoc	310	758	129	149
	3	Croft Ambrey	445	668	129	148
	4	Credenhill	450	445	142	148
	5	Caer Caradoc	477	953	129	137
	6	Sutton Walls	525	464	142	149
	7	Lydney	616	027	156	162
	8	Bredon Hill	958	400	144	150
SP	1	Salmonsbury	173	208	144	163
	2	Chastleton	258	282	144	151
	3	Rainsborough	526	348	145	152
	4	Hunsbury	738	583	133	152
	5	Ivinghoe Beacon	960	168	147	165
SR	1	Bosherston	971	948	151	158
SS	1	Clovelly Dykes	311	234	174	190
	2	Harding's Down	437	906	153	159
	3	Mynydd Bychan	963	756	154	170
ST	1	Hembury Castle	112	031	176	192
	2	Membury	282	028	177	193
	3	Worlebury	314	625	165	182

Fig. 14 Index to Gazetteer (for key see pp. 114–20).
Based upon the Ordnance Survey Map with the
sanction of the Controller of Her Majesty's
Stationery Office, Crown copyright reserved.

ST	4	Llanmelin	460	925	155	171
	5	Almondsbury	596	833	156	172
	6	South Cadbury	628	252	166	183
	7	Bathampton	774	650	156	172
	8	Hambledon Hill	845	126	178	183
	9	Hod Hill	857	106	178	183
	10	Winkelbury	952	217	167	184
SU	1	Yarnbury	035	403	167	184
	2	Casterley	115	535	167	184
	3	Old Sarum	137	327	167	184
	4	Vespasian's Camp	146	417	167	184
	5	Little Woodbury	150	279	167	184
	6	Figsbury Rings	188	338	167	184
	7	Quarley Hill	262	423	167	184
	8	Danebury	323	376	168	185
	9	Bury Hill	346	435	168	185
	10	Beacon Hill	458	572	168	174
	11	Ladle Hill	479	568	168	174
	12	St Catherine's Hill	484	276	168	185
	13	Old Winchester Hill	641	206	168	185
	14	Caesar's Camp, Farnham	825	500	169	186
	15	Caesar's Camp, Easthampstead	863	657	169	175
	16	The Trundle	877	110	181	197
SW	1	Maen Castle	347	257	189	203
	2	Gurnard's Head	433	387	189	203
	3	Chun Castle	405	339	189	203
	4	Carn Brea	686	407	189	203
SX	1	Tregeare Rounds	033	800	185	200
	2	Castle Dore	103	548	186	200
	3	Cranbrook Castle	738	890	175	191
	4	Milber Down	884	698	188	191
SY	1	Blackbury	187	924	176	192
	2	Maiden Castle, Dorset	669	885	178	194
	3	Chalbury	695	838	178	194
	4	Bindon Hill	835	802	178	194
SZ	1	Hengistbury Head	170	908	179	195
	2	Buckland Rings	314	968	180	196
TF	1	Warham	944	409	125	132
TL	1	Ravensburgh	099	295	147	166
	2	Caesar's Camp, Sandy	179	490	147	153

Fig. 15 Index to Gazetteer (for key see pp. 114–20).
Based upon the Ordnance Survey Map with the
sanction of the Controller of Her Majesty's
Stationery Office, Crown copyright reserved.

TL	3	Wandlebury	493 534	148	154
	4	Clare	769 459	149	155
TM	1	Tasburgh	200 960	137	144
TQ	1	Cissbury	139 080	182	198
	2	Chanctonbury Ring	139 120	182	198
	3	Caesar's Camp, Wimbledon	224 711	170	176
	4	Thundersbarrow	229 084	182	198
	5	Hollingbury	322 078	182	198
	6	Caesar's Camp, Keston	421 640	171	177
	7	Ranscombe	438 092	183	198
	8	The Caburn	444 089	183	198
	9	Oldbury	582 566	171	188
	10	East Hill, Hastings	833 099	184	199
TR	1	Bigberry	117 575	173	179
TV	1	Beltout	560 956	183	199

ABERNETHY, *see* **CASTLE LAW.**

ABERYSTWYTH, *see* **PENDINAS.**

ALMONDBURY (fig. 18; Yorks., SE 152 140; 270 metres; pp. 17, 18, pl. 8).

Almost all the earthworks now visible are of the twelfth century AD, but they preserve the lines of earlier ramparts. Their complex history has been unravelled by Professor Varley.

This hill has long been identified convincingly as Camulodunon, the stronghold of Camulos; but the first record of this name dates from the second century AD and Professor Varley has shown that by then the place had been deserted for two centuries or more. The possibility remains that throughout this period tradition had preserved the name used by the original builders, but it is rather more likely that the impressive defences were attributed to a divinity after their actual origin had been forgotten.

The hill was first inhabited in the third millennium BC, but had long been deserted when the first rampart was built. This, termed the univallate enclosure to distinguish it from later more powerful works, took in 1·1 hectares on the south-western half of the hill

1 Tre'r Ceiri, latest phase *(reconstruction)*

2   Maiden Castle from south-east

3   Maiden Castle, East Gateway, phase II *(reconstruction)*

4　Maiden Castle, East Gateway, final phase *(reconstruction)*

5   Tre'r Ceiri, early phase *(reconstruction)*

6   Traprain Law

7   Croft Ambrey, early third century BC *(reconstruction)*